Postdisciplinary Studies in Discourse engages in the exchange between discourse theory and analysis while putting emphasis on the intellectual challenges in discourse research. Moving beyond disciplinary divisions in today's social sciences, the contributions deal with critical issues at the intersections between language and society.

Edited by Johannes Angermuller together with members of DiscourseNet, the series welcomes high-quality manuscripts in discourse research from all disciplinary and geographical backgrounds. DiscourseNet is an international and interdisciplinary network of researchers which is open to discourse analysts and theorists from all backgrounds.

Editorial Board

Cristina Arancibia
Aurora Fragonara
Péter Furkó
Jens Maesse
Eduardo Chávez Herrera
Benno Herzog
Michael Kranert
Jan Krasni
Yannik Porsché
Luciana Radut-Gaghi
Jan Zienkowski

More information about this series at
http://www.palgrave.com/gp/series/14534

Postdisciplinary Studies in Discourse

Series Editor
Johannes Angermuller, Centre for Applied Lingui:
University of Warwick, Coventry, UK

Patrizia Anesa · Aurora Fragonara
Editors

Discourse Processes between Reason and Emotion

A Post-disciplinary Perspective

Editors
Patrizia Anesa
University of Bergamo
Bergamo, Italy

Aurora Fragonara
University of Bergamo
Bergamo, Italy

Postdisciplinary Studies in Discourse
ISBN 978-3-030-70090-4   ISBN 978-3-030-70091-1   (eBook)
https://doi.org/10.1007/978-3-030-70091-1

Contents

Notes on Contributors

Patrizia Anesa is a Researcher in English Language and Translation at the University of Bergamo, Italy. She holds a Ph.D. in English Studies, with a specialization in professional communication. She is a member of the Research Centre on Specialized Languages (CERLIS) and is also an Associate Editor of the IDEA project (International Dialects of English Archive). Her research interests lie mostly in the area of specialized discourse, and she is currently interested in the applications of Conversation Analysis in LSP and the investigation of knowledge asymmetries in expert-lay communication. She is a member of the editorial board of *The International Journal of Law, Language & Discourse.* Patrizia Anesa has also worked extensively in the area of World Englishes and her monograph *Lexical Innovation in World Englishes: Cross-Fertilization and Evolving Paradigms* (2019, London: Routledge) has recently received the 2020 ESSE Book Award.

Ismael Arinas Pellón is a Lecturer in English Communication to engineering students at the Universidad Politécnica de Madrid (UPM), Spain. He has also lectured Business English online courses for CEPADE (online branch of UPM) and Universidad Nacional de Educación a

Distancia (UNED), Spain. His research interests lie essentially in the use of corpus linguistics for genre analysis. More specifically, he has compiled corpora of the following genres in Spanish and English: U.S. patents, technology transfer contracts, legislation on technical issues, legislation on education, annual corporate reports, and online scams. These corpus analyses have focused on identifying the prototypical characteristics of genres, linking phraseology to persuasion strategies, determining the use of interpersonality markers, and studying the relation between vagueness and communication purposes. He is currently participating with an international research group engaged with the development of innovative methods for teaching innovation to university students. His publications cover mostly the following three topics: patents as a genre, persuasion in online scams, and the use of corpora for teaching translation.

Natalia Borza holds a Ph.D. in English Applied Linguistics from Eötvös Loránd University, Budapest. She has worked at the Institute of International Studies and Political Science at Pázmány Péter Catholic University (Hungary), currently as Associate Professor. She has published several register analytical studies investigating the characteristics of academic English. Her research interests embrace discursive legitimation strategies, discursive identity formation, critical discourse analysis of media discourse, and the sociolinguistic aspects of political correctness. At the same time, she has pursued doctoral studies in aesthetics and philosophy, in which fields she has also been actively publishing. Her main fields of academic interest are critical discourse analysis; media discourse; political discourse; and sociolinguistics.

Claire-Anne Ferrière is a Ph.D. student at Lyon 3 University, France. She is interested in the link between language and power in the case of gender relations. She focuses more particularly on feminist texts and discourses challenging established social structures and social practices, in the Critical Discourse Analysis framework. Her Ph.D. thesis focuses on the construction of the latest feminist movement born out of the Weinstein case and on the concept of linguistic community, as well as its limits.

She is a permanent Lecturer at Lyon 3 University, in the language department. She is affiliated to the CEL (Centre d'Études Linguistiques—Corpus, Discours et Société—Linguistics Research Center—Corpus, Discourse and Societies).

Aurora Fragonara is an Adjunct Lecturer in French Language and Linguistics at the University of Bergamo and the University of Milan. She has held a Postdoctoral Researcher position in French Linguistics at the University of Bergamo. She holds a Ph.D. in Linguistics (Science du langage) from the research centre CREM (centre de recherches sur les médiations) at the University of Lorraine. She is still an associated member of that research institution. Her main research interests are French discourse analysis and enunciation theory, combined with cognitive linguistics, pragmatics, and semiotics. She applies this theoretical background to several types of discourses (theatrical, medical, and political), paying a specific attention to the integration of discourse practices in digital media. As a co-editor of a series of proceedings and of a journal issue, she also took part in two scientific research projects on linguistic and pedagogical matters in contemporary second language teaching. She is a member of the DiscourseNet board, where she is in charge of the social media communication and the coordination of the translation process for the website. She is currently carrying out research on argumentation and cognitive biases.

Lyubov Gurevich has been a Faculty Member in the Department of Linguistics and Professional Communication at the Moscow State Linguistic University (Russia) since September 2020. She received her Candidate of Sciences Degree in Philology from Irkutsk State Linguistic University in 2002 and her Doctor of Sciences Degree in Philology from the Military University of the Ministry of Defense of the Russian Federation in 2011. Her current research focuses on cognitive linguistics approaches with a particular interest in pragma-semantic analysis of communication, cognition, and cognitive space dimensions of communication and metacommunication. Her expertise is in pragma-semantic analysis of the interpretant, its cognitive structure, the speaker, and the hearer meaning in communication. Professor Gurevich is actively involved in such professional societies as the Russian Cognitive

Linguists Association, the Russian Academy of Natural History, and the DiscourseNet Association. She is on the editorial board of the journal *Modern Humanities Success* (Russia) and serves on a peer review panel for Publons. She has received several awards for research and academic affairs, including the gold medal of "European Quality" (2013), the diploma of All-Russia Exhibition award winner (2011), and others.

Erica Pinelli is a Research Fellow in Slavic Studies at the University of Pavia, where she teaches Russian language. Her main research interests are Russian linguistics, cognitive linguistics, and political and media discourse.

Azianura Hani Shaari (Ph.D.) is a Senior Lecturer at the Faculty of Social Sciences and Humanities, the National University of Malaysia. Culture, gender, technology, language, and crime are among the research areas that stay close to her heart. She has received several awards for her research in these fields and has been a member of different international projects. She has written several books and has published articles in both local and international journals.

Polina Shvanyukova is an Independent Researcher and Adjunct Lecturer in English Language in the Department of Foreign Language, Literatures and Cultures at the University of Bergamo, Italy. She has held Postdoctoral Researcher positions in English Language and Translation at the Universities of Florence and Bergamo. Her main research interests focus on epistolary discourse and Business English in a historical perspective. She has also published on the history of English language teaching in Italy and Late Modern English travel literature related to the exploration of the Pacific.

Chiara Zanchi is a Postdoc Fellow at University of Pavia, where she teaches language data analysis (M.A. in Linguistics). She is mainly interested in syntax and pragmatics of ancient and modern IE languages.

List of Tables

Gender-Based Violence in Italian Local Newspapers: How Argument Structure Constructions Can Diminish a Perpetrator's Responsibility

Post-disciplinary Approaches to Discourse Analysis

Patrizia Anesa and Aurora Fragonara

1 Introduction

This volume is a collection of studies which address different forms of discourse by focusing on the emergence of power dynamics in communication and their importance in shaping the production and reception of messages. In particular, drawing on the consideration that, from a quantitative perspective, the production and circulation of (relatively) new messages have dramatically increased in recent years (especially because of new technologies that facilitate self-expression as well as the spreading of ideas and content), this collection offers an investigation of discursive

P. Anesa (✉) · A. Fragonara
University of Bergamo, Bergamo, Italy
e-mail: patrizia.anesa@unibg.it

A. Fragonara
e-mail: aurora.fragonara@guest.unibg.it

© The Author(s), under exclusive license to Springer Nature
Switzerland AG 2021
P. Anesa and A. Fragonara (eds.), *Discourse Processes between Reason
and Emotion*, Postdisciplinary Studies in Discourse,
https://doi.org/10.1007/978-3-030-70091-1_1

productions related to 'old' and 'new' media, with particular attention devoted to digital products.

The contributions focus on specific cognitive aspects, such as the verbal expression of reasoning or emotions, as well as on linguistic and discursive processes (e.g. lexical and syntactic choices or pragmatic features of communication). The interaction between reasoning, feelings, and emotions is applied, to different degrees and in different modes, to several fields of discourse where power dynamics may emerge. These include political, corporate, media, pedagogical, and academic discourse, and this volume aims to include representative instances of this heterogeneity.

More specifically, some of the topics addressed in this volume include, inter alia, argumentation (up to manipulation), storytelling, and the linguistic construction of empathy. These topics apply to reasoning as well as to emotional and affective dimensions of the self, and thus, reasoning and emotions are often combined in the process of understanding or making a specific reality understandable. By means of an example, storytelling combines the importance of logical structures (such as the conception of a story as a whole and the cause-effect relationship which grounds the transforming process within a story) with the arousal of emotions and feelings. These dynamics often emerge through some form of empathy with one or more characters or, conversely, through the development of negative feelings generated by the presence of unlikeable or problematic characters. Within this framework, empathy can also be taken into account as a specific way to analyse the relationship between discourse and power from a linguistic and cognitive perspective. In particular, it is via empathy that individuals can embrace the viewpoint of their addressees; that is, they can look at a given situation through the perceptions and/or feelings of their interlocutors, and consequently, discursive and linguistic markers of this mental operation are found in their verbal productions. Conversely, the lack of empathic attitudes may hinder these processes significantly.

As will be seen, this volume is deeply rooted, both theoretically and methodologically, in the acknowledgement that the investigation of the complex interaction between reason and emotion in discursive productions cannot be exempt from the adoption of a multi-disciplinary perspective. Without this perspective, the investigation runs the risk of oversimplifications which would neglect the intricacy of discourse processes and practices.

2   Structure of the Volume

This volume purposefully brings together different strands of scholarship with diverse intellectual provenance, and thus, the different contributions attempt to transcend fixed boundaries of research and offer multi-perspectival views on various discursive phenomena.

This introductory chapter illustrates the key theoretical and methodological frameworks, which are adopted in this volume by the different contributors, with the common aim to analyse the complex relations which develop between emotion and reason when observing language in use. Discourse Analysis (DA) at large is here seen as a broad and multifaceted research area which can help us to understand hierarchical relations and participants' positions in different discourse fields. The main approaches adopted in the studies included in this collection range from Critical Discourse Analysis (CDA) to Corpus Linguistics (CL), and from semantic-pragmatic frameworks to communication ones. In addition, a single contribution will often draw on a combination of multiple theoretical and methodological slants. This variety confirms the need to adopt a multi-perspectival, or rather post-perspectival, approach to discourse and the necessity to go beyond strict disciplinary boundaries with the aim to delve into complex discursive dynamics. Thus, we may argue that this collection stems from the awareness that traditional disciplinary categories need to be considered from a more fluid viewpoint in order to gain a deeper understanding of the complex processes which characterize language in/as social action.

The first part of the book focuses specifically on message processing. The opening chapter of this section, by Lyubov Gurevich, offers a pragma-semantic analysis of defamatory communication. This analysis takes into account three cognitive space dimensions (gender, age, and structure) and shows possible interpretations of male, female, and children's discourse by drawing on the example of gossip. It observes how the type of observer in metacommunication determines a given perlocutionary effect, influences the choice of specific verbs of defamation, and defines the possibility of defamatory metacommunication within discourse. The study suggests that the variability of pragma-semantic meanings of defamatory lexemes is determined by such intralinguistic reasons as blurred concept and extralinguistic reasons as dependence on different dimensions of cognitive space. Drawing on Bateson (2002), the author argues that defamatory communication is better comprehended and interpreted as 'communication about communication' (Bateson, 2002), or metacommunication, in which the correlation of communicative roles influences the meanings of utterances and their perlocutionary effect. It is an integrative approach to the investigation of the pragmatic component of a defamatory utterance which influences the stability of the meaning of a lexeme. Thus, it can strengthen the negative connotation of a defamatory lexeme or, conversely, neutralize it in discourse.

The section on message processing is concluded by the chapter authored by Patrizia Anesa, Ismael Arinas Pellón, and Azianura Hani Shaari, entitled 'Exploiting irrational evaluations: The discursive features of scams across genres'. This work focuses on scams as a discursive product and on the cognitive and linguistic processes which determine their success. This chapter observes which persuasion strategies pertain to different types of scams, by analysing a multi-genre corpus which includes '419 frauds' (also known as 'advance-fee frauds') and 'romance scams'. In particular, the analysis illustrates the type of discursive devices which are employed to attract the victims' interest and subsequent trust, to the extent that the victim then becomes unable to recognize the signs which constitute clear manifestations of fraud. Indeed, persuasion is a core aspect of human interaction which, in the case of scams, represents a highly manipulative tool (Ferreira, 2016: 29). The hypothesis tested is that the two different types of scams draw considerably on errors of judgement. More specifically, the reading of errors of judgement provided is indebted to Lea et al. (2009), and their taxonomy, including motivational and cognitive judgement errors (2009: 25–34), is used to identify the persuasive processes adopted by the scammers in order to construct narratives which display a high level of credibility.

The second section of the volume takes a closer look at the dynamics of power in given discursive representations of social actions. It is opened by Claire-Anne Ferrière's chapter, which deals with legitimation seen through the lens of the new feminist movement. This work describes the rhetorical and pragmatic tools that women in the new feminist movement use to enter this power struggle, weaving together reason and emotion to support their claims. In particular, it compares texts from two major stages in the development of the movement, i.e. the recent Weinstein sexual assault case and the January 2018s Women's March. The analysis illustrates how women manage to convince their audience of the legitimacy of their claims and progressively construct a common, alternative narrative about gendered power relations.

The following chapter is by Natalia Borza and describes the discursive representation of violence in the context of the migration crisis. More specifically, it investigates the emergence of the culture of non-violence in the English-speaking media reporting on the so-called Chemnitz events (Friese et al., 2019), in which anti-migrant demonstrations were sparked by the fatal stabbing of a German citizen by three immigrants in Chemnitz, eastern Germany, in 2018. The analysis focuses on newspaper articles reporting on an anti-racism rock concert which was held in response to the demonstrations. Drawing on CDA, the study explores the narrative recontextualization of the Chemnitz events in online English language articles drawn from four different sources (the *BBC*, *The Guardian*, *The Telegraph*, and *The Times*). This chapter represents a qualitative case study on how a lexical field (Fowler, 1991) is created around the theme of violence, in order to promote the culture of non-violence. The analysis applies van Leeuwen's (2008) socio-semantic inventory of the discursive representations of social actors and social actions. The patterns of social agent inclusion versus exclusion (by way of suppression or backgrounding), and that of social action activation versus deactivation (by way of nominalization or descriptivization), are analysed through the examination of the linguistic features of the discursive representation of violence in the texts. The findings suggest that the articles encourage social action within the frame of non-violence by providing an unbalanced representation of social actors and by over-representing the deactivation of social actions.

The theme of violence is also investigated by Chiara Zanchi and Erica Pinelli who, in their chapter 'Gender-Based Violence in Italian Local Newspapers: How Argument Structure Constructions Can Diminish a Perpetrator's Responsibility', focus on the theme of gender-based violence (GBV) in local Italian newspapers and observe how argument structure constructions can diminish perpetrators' responsibility. More specifically, through both a qualitative and a quantitative analysis, this chapter discusses how argument structure constructions are used in Italian newspapers to represent GBV events and how such usage affects the attribution of responsibility through the suppression, backgrounding, or eventuation of the perpetrator (Tranchese & Zollo, 2013). The main background assumption is twofold: firstly, transitivity is the foundation of event representation (Fowler, 1991: 71), and secondly, constructions are meaningful. The findings show that constructional choices prompt different viewpoints covering the same event (Goldberg, 1995), and can bias our perception towards seeing either participant as the primary actor of such events (Bohner, 2001; Henley et al., 1995).

Aurora Fragonara's chapter, entitled 'The Ethos of the Spokesperson: A Populist Attempt to Create an Empathic Connection', continues with the investigation of digital discourse and focuses on the key role of the spokesperson in the digital era. Populism being a 'thin ideology' (Engesser et al., 2017), characterized by a prominence of emotional expression over argumentation, the production of social media content by populist political figures, requires careful structuring in order to appear substantial, especially given the limited amount of characters permitted by platforms such as Twitter. In this respect, cognitive science has shown how storytelling is regarded as a mental process used to make sense of, and order out of, human experience (Turner, 1996). The analysis is carried out on a bilingual corpus comprised of tweets by two European politicians regarded as populists, Nigel Farage (writing in English) and Marine LePen (writing in French). Through a combination of Discourse Analysis (Maingueneau, 2014), enunciative frameworks (Benveniste, 1966; Kerbrat-Orecchioni, 2009), and Cognitive Linguistics (Fauconnier & Turner, 2002), selected discursive markers, common to the two languages, have been analysed. They include, in particular, verbs of actions or feelings and the use of the pronoun *we*. Results show that storytelling works here as a framework to encode and express a specific point of view on current events and socio-political issues through verbs and expressions of general and universal sensations or feeling which the intended audience can easily relate to.

'Of Emotion Terms and E-Implicatures: An Exploratory Study of the Explicit and Implicit Emotional Dimensions in a Corpus of Newsletters in English' is the concluding chapter by Polina Shvanyukova. It moves to a different field of analysis, that of teaching, and the investigation is carried out by adopting a case study approach. The study takes into account the ELT (English Language Teaching) and Applied Linguistics community, as represented by one of the best-known international English language teacher associations, the International Association of Teachers of English as a Foreign Language (IATEFL). This chapter examines the ways in which emotional language is used to offer advice to peer practitioners and novice teachers in newsletters published by the IATEFL. The focus is on the specific language resources and rhetorical strategies employed by practitioners addressing their peers, not only to formulate the content in a way which can be easily understood, but also to engage and persuade their audience by triggering an emotional response.

3 Implications for Post-disciplinary Discourse Approaches

The contributions to this volume draw on inter-disciplinary, trans-disciplinary, and post-disciplinary approaches to Discourse Analysis. DA is, of course, variously defined but since its beginning the analysis of language in use has been based on the interrelation and interdependence of different disciplines, often stemming from diverse theoretical and methodological backgrounds (see Fairclough & Wodak, 1997; van Dijk, 1997; Wodak, 2001). Moreover, it has long been acknowledged that DA has generally involved multiple areas of research such as linguistics, sociology, anthropology, ethnography, psychology, rhetorics, semiotics, statistics, history, and politics. In addition, in recent decades, disciplines such as computer science, digital humanities, or media studies have also made a substantial contribution to the field.

The plurality of approaches allows an opening up of the discussion and thus can enhance innovation. The *fil rouge* among them may be summarized in the awareness that 'discourse is socially constitutive as well as socially conditioned' (Fairclough & Wodak, 1997: 258), and multiple perspectives need to be adopted in order to grasp its complexities.

In many respects, DA is deeply rooted in inter- and trans-disciplinarity, and researchers have also gradually acknowledged the relevance of post-disciplinarity to discourse studies, although this aspect still remains undervalued. Regardless of the specific methodological frameworks which may aim to understand, explain, or substantiate discourse phenomena, and despite the approaches adopted (be they more nomothetic or idiographic, quantitative or qualitative, descriptive or prescriptive, contemplative or action-oriented), the analysis of discourse can benefit from the overcoming of static disciplinary categories.

One may argue that, given its genealogy, DA has always developed without a sole theoretical framework and is inherently post-disciplinary. While it is clear that it is somehow a decentred area, acknowledging the importance of post-disciplinarity is a key element to guarantee a constant revitalization of the field. In other words, it may be a truism to say that DA was already post-disciplinary before its very definition as such. However, gaining an awareness of the implications that this approach brings with it is crucial for the soundness of any scientific approach within the area.

Post-disciplinarity has developed along the lines of closely-related concepts, but it has assumed slightly different contours. In particular, pluri(multi-)disciplinarity tends to be seen as the coexistence of different disciplines which somehow preserve an independent nature. Inter-disciplinarity is generally defined as the development of an integrative framework, thus potentially creating new theoretical (often holistic) approaches. Post-disciplinary perspectives do not necessarily equal but do, to some extent, enhance the reconciliation of diverse epistemic communities and the aggregation of isolated specializations. From this viewpoint, post-disciplinarity should not be confused with eclecticism or a lack of systematicity, but is intended here as a plurality of views transcending fixed categories in order to integrate more dynamic and fluid frameworks which can be adapted to the peculiarities of different phenomena. Thus, it represents a form of 'plural synthesis' in which the methods traditionally associated with one discipline (e.g. statistics) can also benefit a different area of studies (e.g. sociology) in a reciprocal 'contamination' in which the original distinctions appear less functional than the action that they aim to perform.

The overarching view adopted in this volume does not correspond to a multifaceted perspective intended as the piling up of different methods and theories, but is rather about their transformation into new schemas which can serve specific research purposes. This attempt to move beyond fixed categories does not claim to be more complete or comprehensive than other approaches, but is simply functional to the investigation of the complex ontology of discursive phenomena through a pragmatic and constructive synthesis. Such synthesis is not based merely on the combination of different viewpoints, but on their interdependence and reciprocal influence.

This is not to deny the existence and the usefulness of canonical disciplinary categories; rather, the aim is to acknowledge that, in order to understand, explain, and substantiate language in action comprehensively, we often need the adoption of a synthetic perspective which overcomes simplistic generalizations and ritual replications. In this view, a post-disciplinary approach does not ignore the existence of disciplines, nor does it argue for abstinence from clear theoretical and methodological constructs, but rather it transcends them in order to provide finely articulated ways to reconcile differences and stimulate discussion. In other words, it attempts to mediate and synthesize theories, practices, and strategies which traditionally belong to specific areas of research.

'Inter-disciplinarity', 'trans-disciplinarity', 'multi-disciplinarity', and 'post-disciplinarity' have often been labelled as opportunist approaches. A certain degree of pragmatism is, of course, an essential component of a framework which aims to go beyond fixed borders in order to answer specific questions. However, the vitality of post-disciplinarity can enhance the evolution of traditional paradigms, where the notion of specialization and that of transcendence of disciplines are not mutually exclusive but, conversely, nourish each other by offering novel ways of tackling issues, especially those of a social nature. Thus, different paradigms do not only coexist, but may mutually enrich.

A word of caution is of course necessary, in that fluid and dynamic approaches may clearly impact scholarly standards and may ignore the specificities of the context in which they developed. All the same, this synthetic view is particularly beneficial to the stimulation of deep reflection if the weight of academic traditions and intellectual legacies is acknowledged and scholars manage to utilize these encounters with such traditions and to capitalize on the mutual benefits which such confrontations can generate.

This synthetic approach can limit the fragmentation of research trends and the related centrifugal tendencies. Moreover, it can provide fertile ground for the cross-validation of lines of inquiry, the reciprocal stimulation of intellectual input, and the expansion of scholarly horizons. From this perspective, the importance of having well-defined lines of research within disciplines (Eadie, 2011; Nordenstreng, 2011) is not neglected; on the contrary, being able to move such boundaries can spawn new theoretical and empirical questions, generated by the paradigmatic shift towards multi-perspective analysis, which acknowledges the mutual and specific contribution of several disciplines in decoding discourse phenomena.

References

Bateson, G. (2002). *Mind and nature: A necessary unity*. New York: Hampton Press.

Benveniste, É. (2011/1966). *Problèmes de linguistique générale* (tome I). Paris: Gallimard.

Bohner, G. (2001). Writing about rape: Use of the passive voice and other distancing text features as an expression of perceived responsibility of the victim. *British Journal of Social Psychology, 40,* 515–529.

Eadie, W. F. (2011). Stories we tell: Fragmentation and convergence in communication disciplinary history. *Review of Communication, 11*(3), 161–176.

Engesser, S., Ernst, N., Esser, F., & Büchel, F. (2017). Populism and social media: How politicians spread a fragmented ideology. *Information, Communication & Society, 20*(8), 1109–1126.

Fairclough, N., & Wodak, R. (1997). Critical discourse analysis. In T. van Dijk (Ed.), *Discourse studies: A multidisciplinary introduction* (Vol. 2, pp. 258–284). London: Sage.

Fauconnier, G., & Turner, M. (2002). *The way we think*. New York: Basic books.

Ferreira, A. (2016). Persuasion in Scams. In M. Jakobsson (Ed.), *Understanding social engineering based scams*. New York: Springer-Verlag.

Fowler, R. (1991). *Language in the news: Discourse and ideology in the press*. London: Routledge.

Friese, H., Nolden, M., & Schreiter, M. (2019). *Rassismus im Alltag. Theoretische und empirische Perspektiven nach Chemnitz*. Bielefeld: Transcript.

Goldberg, A. E. (1995). *Constructions: A construction grammar approach to argument structure*. Chicago: University of Chicago Press.

Henley, N. M., Miller, M., & Beazley, J. A. (1995). Syntax, semantics, and sexual violence: Agency and the passive voice. *Journal of Language and Social Psychology, 14*(1/2), 60–84.

Kawai, K. (1950). Mokusatsu, Japan's response to the Potsdam Declaration. *Pacific Historical Review, 19*(4), 409–414.

Kerbrat-Orecchioni, C. (2009). *L'énonciation. De la subjectivité dans le langage*. Paris: Armand Colin.

Lea, S., Fischer, P., & Evans, K. (2009). *The psychology of scams: Provoking and committing errors of judgment*. Exeter: Office of Fair Trading.

Maingueneau, D. (2014). *Discours et analyse du discours*. Paris: Armand Colin.

Nordenstreng, K. (2011). Lost in abundance? Reflections on disciplinarity. In B. Zelizer (Ed.), *Making the university matter* (pp. 194–205). New York, NY: Routledge.

Tranchese, A., & Zollo, S. A. (2013). The construction of gender-based violence in the British printed and broadcast media. *Critical Approaches to Discourse Analysis Across Disciplines, 7*(1), 141–163.

Turner, M. (1996). *The literary mind, the origins of thought and language*. New York and Oxford: Oxford University Press.

van Dijk, T. A. (1995). Aims of critical discourse analysis. *Japanese Discourse, 1*, 17–27.

van Dijk, T. A. (Ed.). (1997). *Discourse studies: A multidisciplinary introduction* (2 Vols.). London: Sage.

van Leeuwen, T. (2008). *Discourse and practice: New tools for critical discourse analysis*. Oxford: Oxford University Press.

Wodak, R. (2001). What CDA is about—A summary of its history, important concepts and its developments. In R. Wodak & M. Meyer (Eds.), *Methods of critical discourse analysis* (pp. 1–13). London: Sage.

Defamatory Communication via Cognitive Space Dimensions Analysis: Pragma-Semantic Approach

Lyubov Gurevich

1 Introduction

By definition, defamatory communication utterances tend to injure people's reputation and often become the reason why those people are regarded with such unpleasant feelings as contempt, derision, discredit and even hatred (Defamatory Communication Law and Legal Definition, 2019). As a consequence, the defamation law, which has been enacted in almost all civilized societies recently, must deal with *libels* (written defamatory statements) and *slanders* (spoken or oral defamatory statements). The major part of defamatory utterances belongs to that category per se, but some of the utterances require proof of their insulting nature regarding the reason that defamation can be implied, but not explicitly communicated in the utterance. Given the huge demand, expert semantic-textual examination has become a common

L. Gurevich (✉)
Department of Foreign Languages and Intercultural Communication,
Moscow State Linguistic University, Moscow, Russia

© The Author(s), under exclusive license to Springer Nature
Switzerland AG 2021
P. Anesa and A. Fragonara (eds.), *Discourse Processes between Reason
and Emotion*, Postdisciplinary Studies in Discourse,
https://doi.org/10.1007/978-3-030-70091-1_2

practice in numerous litigation cases. It is beyond argument that it would hardly become the reason of prior importance in the fundamental research development in this area, but the fact is that basic studies have already been practically applied in the social sphere, namely in the areas of human interaction and communication regulation. The problem of defamatory communication has become a topical subject matter, both in social interaction practice and in scientific research.

The interest in the retrieval of hidden meanings from the utterances is concordant with reported findings for the "explicature / implicature" and "implicature / implication" distinction which arises for semantics / pragmatics theorizing (Carston, 2012: 2). There is a fundamental difference between: (a) what the sentence explicates and what is not articulated in words; (b) what the sentence implies and the Speaker implicates; and (c) what the Speaker implies and the Hearer infers (Austin, 1962; Searle, 1969). In the light of this difference, the foundational scientific outlooks on the utterance pragmatics have been partially reconsidered, and novel approaches, such as the Neo-Gricean Pragmatic Theory of Conversational Implicature (Kecskes & Horn, 2007), Relevance Theory (Carston, 2002, 2006; Carston & Powell, 2004; Wilson & Sperber, 2004; etc.) and Cognitive Space Theory (Peverelli, 2000, etc.), have appeared.

Consequently, the necessity of the pragma-semantic approach has recently become urgent in the analysis of people's communication. Scholars are attempting to discover the viable methodology of implicative meaning retrieval from the utterance and to disclose hidden indexicals of pragmatic meaning (Carston, 2002, 2006, 2012; Sperber & Wilson, 1985, 1995, 1998, 2002; Wilson, 2003; Bateson, 2002; Bach, 2006 and others).

My inferential approach to pragmatics is partially based upon the Gricean Pragmatic Theory (Grice, 1975), the pioneer of which introduced the notion of conversational implicature to demonstrate how "the speaker meaning", which is not directly encoded in the words, can be decoded (or inferred) by the Hearer in conversation. However, Grice describes an *almost ideal communicative situation* where conversational exchange is based on four basic conversational maxims explaining all possible cooperative efforts of its interlocutors (Grice, 1969). As Wilson and Sperber argue, the implicature explanation needs "cognitively realistic terms" which "might contribute to an empirically plausible account of comprehension" (Wilson & Sperber, 2004: 2). Presumably, for that reason, some aspects of his account have been questioned by theorists who share Grice's intuition at a fundamental level (Carston, 2002, 2012; Félix-Brasdefer, 2020; Wilson & Sperber, 2004, etc.).

I share Wilson and Sperber's viewpoint relating to the existence of external stimuli that provide inputs to the cognitive processes of individuals (Wilson & Sperber, 2004: 2), which correlate with Schlesinger, Meadows, Peverelli and others' theorizing; indeed, these scholars have shed new light on the complex relationship between cognitive and linguistic categories in the communication process (Meadows, Meadows, Randers, & Behrens, 1972; Peverelli, 2000; Schlesinger, 1995; etc.). I basically rely upon their approach, which supposes that each individual possesses his / her own unique *individual cognitive space* (i.e. *an individual perceptive capacity*) which depends on incoming information, as well as the person's life experience and awareness, conditioned by the cultural settings of his / her lingua-culture (i.e. *collective cognitive space*).

From this perspective, some language categories can be composed with the help of more primitive cognitive notions, which were termed by Schlesinger as *cognitive dimensions*. He applied this approach to the study of the category of case, and his followers researched human perspectives mapping in several cognitive spaces within three cognitive space dimensions. My research is a further attempt to apply the cognitive space dimensions approach in the analysis of defamatory communication and metacommunication within cognitive space dimensions such as *Gender*, *Age* and *Structure*. Cognitive space dimensions act here as extralinguistic factors of communication which serve as vectors of proposition deflection in the process of interpretation.

Due to the above-described specificity of the cognitive space dimensions approach, my research is also based on Morris's foundations of semiotics, where the process of interpretation (or semiosis) is represented in its broader sense, where additional components—the interpretant and the interpreter—are included. The interpreter is regarded as an integral component of the process of interpretation. The "interpretant" is classed as a part of a person's communicative behaviour—a combination of two different entities: (1) the sign designating the utterer's meaning and (2) the sign designating the interpreter's perception and comprehension (Morris, 1946).

Subsequently, the scientific idea of inferential pragmatics, whose goal is "to explain how the hearer infers the speaker's meaning on the basis of the evidence provided" (Wilson & Sperber, 2004), is additionally based on Peirce's and Morris's theoretical approaches (Morris, 1946; Pierce, 1994, 1997) and on the foundation of the causal theory of perception put forth by Grice (1961).

All of the above-described theories underpin my research and support the basic ideas of Peverelli's Cognitive Space Approach.

2   Cognitive Space Approach

The basics of Peverelli's Cognitive Space Approach stem from Dongen's Theory of Social Integration and Weick's Theory of Reducing Equivocality in processes of social interaction. The notion of cognitive space was borrowed by Weick from Fauconnier's model of Mental Space, whose concepts were reinterpreted as "social-cognitive configuration and multiple inclusion".

According to Peverelli, there are two basic elements in a cognitive space which are closely interconnected in interpersonal communication. They are: (1) "the social element, the actors involved, and (2) the cognitive element, their share cognitive matter" (Benking, 2019). The shared cognitive matter can also be referred to as "collective cognitive space", which helps people understand each other while communicating. The shared content can include symbols, shared views, common language use, social norms and common ways to do things. But there is another cognitive space, which is not shared with anybody else. It utterly and completely belongs to the individual. It is his / her life experience, education, worldview, personal identity, etc. (Meadows et al., 1972; Schlesinger, 1995). It is termed "individual cognitive space", which acts like a filter of input information in the communication act (Gurevich, 2009: 9). It means that people from different backgrounds (individual cognitive space) comprehend the same situation differently and assess it in their own way. In other words, implicature, which is formed and conveyed by the Speaker and perceived by the Hearer in his / her own specific way, becomes that unstable component of the utterance's pragmatic meaning, depending, to the fullest extent, on the interlocutors' individual cognitive spaces correlation.

The other actual reason why the cognitive space approach is considered to be appropriate for the analysis of the utterance pragmatics is that the para- and extralinguistic content of the utterance prevails over articulated content. According to Grof, human communication is a very complex process, which comprises not only verbal exchange but also a variety of kinetic and paralinguistic elements. "These can be seen as metacommunicative signals, or messages about messages, indicating how the verbal communication should be understood and interpreted" (Grof, 1964: 128). The utterance meaning is not a literal verbal meaning; it is a critical codetermination based on the analysis of many paralinguistic signals. A third of the meaning, or even less, is transferred from the spoken words in verbal communication (O'Rourke, 2008: 216), and presumably, the major part of this transferred meaning is dependent on its extralinguistic factors.

The inference of the utterance meaning by the Hearer is dependent on numerous factors, which stem from the person's reflection of the social realm in his / her mind. This means that the structure and the essence of cognitive dimensions, which help the Hearer to infer the Speaker meaning, can differ from one communicative act to another. Consequently, it is difficult for the meaning to be described and structured within the rigid framework of a universal theory. This article represents an experimental research piece based on the analysis of certain communicative acts, while it also seeks to demonstrate how cognitive space dimensions analysis can help to comprehend the peculiarity of the speech interpretation process.

3   Cognitive Structure of Metacommunication

3.1   Why Metacommunication?

I have intuitively chosen metacommunicative predicates for the analysis of the Hearer meaning in the utterance due to their structural complexity. Paradoxically, this complex cognitive structure of metacommunicative predicates facilitates comprehension of the Hearer utterance inference due to the fact that the explication of the Speaker meaning and its inference by the Hearer is already contained in the cognitive structure of the verb and partially in its semantics (for correlation of the cognitive and semantic structures of the word, see Gurevich, 2009). In order to understand what is implied by this assumption, let us consider the cognitive essence of metacommunication and a metacommunicative predicate.

It is necessary to point out that the notion of metacommunication has not yet been distinguished, and scholars tend to interpret it differently (see Gurevich, 2009). I follow the interpretation of Watzlawick (1967) and Lenz (1997), according to which metacommunication is termed "communication about communication" (Lenz, 1997). Thus, a metacommunicative predicate contains the reference to two communicative acts in its cognitive structure and additionally the Speaker's judgement of the first communicative act. Let us now consider it in detail.

The cognitive structure of metacommunication contains two communicative acts which can be termed: (1) a precedent communicative situation (act) and (2) a current communicative situation (act). When we try to analyse the meaning of the utterance *John insulted Tom* (a current communicative situation [CCS]), we can infer that there was another, abusive by its nature, precedent communicative situation (PCS)—for instance, when *John called Tom an idiot* (pejorative phrase). To be more exact, the precedent communicative situation was in the form of a dialogue where the Speaker (John) addressed the Hearer (Tom) with the phrase: "*What an idiot you are!*".

The metacommunicative predicate *insulted* specifies not only the existence of PCS, but also the pejorative character of the Speaker$_1$ utterance.

It is the Hearer$_1$ meaning, and the Hearer$_1$ becomes the Speaker$_2$ in the following communicative situation, i.e. in the CCS.

The Speaker and the Hearer meanings are not directly interdependent and equal by their content. According to Horn, the Speaker exploits pragmatic principles in conveying his utterance, relying on the Hearer's ability and intention to invoke the same principles in the process of interpretation (Horn, 2006: 4; Horn & Ward, 2004). This means that the Speaker meaning depends, to a large extent, on his / her personal mental abilities and the communicative situation's peculiarity. The instability and uncertainty of the Hearer meaning also stem from the lack of information or the meaning's partial representation of the perlocutionary effect on the Hearer. We can anticipate the meaning, or reason based on premises, but it is not going to become a fact; our assertion will always be in the status of supposition.

The cognitive structure of the metacommunicative predicate incorporates information from both communicative situations and speech act assessment, which often (not always) represent a Hearer meaning. The role of the Hearer$_1$ (CCS) does not always coincide with the role of the Speaker$_2$ (PCS); the second role can belong to the Observer of the PCS. This means that someone witnessed the dialogue where John called Tom an idiot and described it in the CCS, having used the metacommunicative predicate *insulted*.

The assessment component of the semantic structure of the metacommunicative predicate can be considered as the explicature of the Hearer meaning, which is why we analyse it within the framework of cognitive space structure and in terms of cognitive space dimensions.

The basic cognitive space dimensions of defamatory metacommunication in our analysis are Gender, Age and Structure. We have not chosen these cognitive dimensions deliberately; they revealed themselves during the pragmatic analysis of the numerous examples of defamatory utterances from the COCA and BNC corpuses. These cognitive dimensions have proved themselves as above-described vectors of input information deflection. They have manifested different pragmatic content in similar contexts. There can be conceivably some other additional cognitive dimensions, which can be revealed by further analysis. Their number is not limited or restricted by the research, but presumably the language functioning process can become their natural constraint.

3.2   Gender Dimension of Cognitive Space

The research matter for the article totalled more than 1,000 samples, retrieved from the British National Corpus (BNC) and the Corpus of Contemporary American English (COCA). The core elements of utterances were the defamatory metacommunication predicates of *gossip, slander, humiliation*, etc. The lexeme *gossip (gossiping)* has been taken as an example of the research analysis in this chapter to demonstrate how the gender dimension of cognitive space of defamatory metacommunication is used in its interpretation.

Interestingly enough, the analysis of the metacommunicative lexeme of gossip has revealed that the female discourse is predominantly associated with sharing of negative information and withholding of positive information on the others. The couplets, accompanying a metacommunicative lexeme, are engaged in negative projection:

(1) *Bad Girls are more likely to accept gossiping, bullying and aggressive behavior in their own lives (N. Jensen. The sisters).*

On the assumption that the logical-grammatical meanings of homogenous parts of the sentence represent uniformity and repeatability of the lexical concept (Babaitseva & Maksimov, 1987), it is arguable that the couplets of the metacommunicative lexeme *gossiping*, consisting of the lexemes *bullying* and *aggressive behavior*, complement their shared conceptual framework of aggressive communication. These couplets tend to aggravate the negative perlocutionary effect on the Hearer.

Sometimes the negative utterance assertion is articulated in the sentence following the defamatory metacommunicative lexeme:

(2) *Then you can see them from 9:30 am to 11:00 am drinking coffee with their friends (who are also housewives), gossiping, criticizing the neighbors ("Why a woman's age at time of marriage matters, and what this tells").*

This detailing of the utterance's propositional component, on the one hand, justifies the assessment of the PCS as *gossiping*; on the other hand, it intensifies the negative connotation[1] of the metacommunicative lexeme, as can be observed in such couplets as *spreading rumors* and *gossiping*.

The propositional component of the utterance can be described sketchily, without detailing, and represents almost a neutral description of a situation which took place in the past (it becomes the topic of the metacommunicative utterance), but the denotation of two women talking as gossiping creates an implicature of something indecent, or even obscene:

(3) *"Mona is not seen in a few episodes until she appears in "The Badass Seed," gossiping with Hanna about her morning shower with Caleb"* (Pretty Little Liars).

The explication of the negative assertion of the PCS content can be achieved in indirect speech, followed by the lexeme *gossiping*:

(4) *I will be interested if, you know, how your babysitter feels if you find her gossiping about you and saying, oh, you know, she just doesn't want to be home with her kid or something of that sort (Spok. Tell Me More).*

The reason why the Observer (and simultaneously the Speaker of the CCS) reproduces the content of the PCS is presumably the same as in the previously-analysed examples. Nevertheless, the lexeme *gossiping*, followed by the indirect speech component, containing explication of the content of gossiping, is not understood as lexical overabundance. The latter serves as the explicature of the negative implied meaning of the defamatory lexeme.

The analysis of female defamatory metacommunication discourse, on the one hand, proves the instability of the defamatory lexemes' linguistic

---

[1] I use Turansky's definition of the term "intensifier" here, according to which any means of increasing the degree of the utterance's expressiveness can be considered to be an intensifier (Turansky, 2006). Semanticheskaya kategoriya intensivnosti v angliiskom yazyike (Semantic Category of Intensiveness in English) (Moscow: Vysshaya Shkola).

meaning: they need contextual support of the meaning in the form of couplets or explicitating clauses, conveyed in the utterance. In other words, the lexeme *gossip* needs explication or additional information about whether it is neutral small talk or a blistering tirade. On the other hand, it demonstrates a more injurious and destructive effect of the female utterance in comparison with male or self-referential discourse. As Coie states, "women are also more likely to express aggressive feelings by gossiping and spreading false rumors" (Coie, Terry, Lenox, Lochman, & Hyman, 1995).

The self-referential discourse of gossiping, by contrast, regardless of the Speaker's gender, is rather neutral than emphatic:

(5) *However, telling stuff to my best friends wasn't gossiping, it was data sharing (M. Marks. Forget me knot).*

The male discourse of gossip, on the contrary, tends to be less negative in its nature. The assessment component in it is mostly neutral:

(6) *Shuffling swarms of excited people, oblivious of the chill in the air, leaned into one another, gossiping, chatting, glancing toward the Hunterdon County Courthouse that dominated the small-town street (E. Ifkovic. FIC: Cold Morning: An Edna Ferber Mystery).*

The couplets *gossiping*, *chatting* and *glancing* prove not to contain any negative connotation. They complement their shared conceptual framework of "innocent tattling". That framework is a listing of neutrally-coloured lexemes, which tend to neutralize the suppositional negative assertion conveyed by the participle *gossiping*.

The male defamatory discourse of gossip is seldom used with negatively-marked attributes or couplets, if to compare it with female discourse. Confer:

(7) *If he was in a hurry, it was a short conversation; if he had time to gossip, then we gossiped (male discourse);* and
(8) *The victim comes into view behind the gossiping students as a popular song about rumors swells in the background. The subsequent section*

of the story features the moment in which the girl learns she is the topic of lunchtime conversation" (C. Kelly. The Cafeteria as Contact Zone: Developing a Multicultural Perspective through Multilingual and Multimodal Literacies) (female discourse).

The latter example demonstrates a negative perlocutionary effect, conveyed by the lexeme *victim,* serving here as a negative assessment component of the whole utterance.

The use of the lexeme *gossip,* with attributes containing negative connotations (e.g. *malicious gossip*) or in homogeneous parts of the sentence (e.g. "psychological bullying" such as *gossiping, spreading rumours, and shunning or exclusion*), proves that the negative assessment component is not integrated into the lexical meaning of the lexeme *gossip*; it is part of its pragmatics. Thus, "negativity" is not embedded in the word semantics; it is not a characteristic feature of connotation, but rather is an interlocutor's association, which comes to people's mind due to their individual conceptualization of this phenomenon. The interlocutors tend to assess the other people's talk, using the same lexeme *gossip* with different implications. Consequently, the pragmatic meaning of this lexeme varies greatly in different contexts, thus demonstrating its instability and diffuseness.

The instability of the pragmatic component of defamatory metacommunicative predicates is also confirmed by the fact that the general assessment of gossip in social discourse is rather neutral, as if to disregard its gender dimension. The research proves that the academic and mass media discourse definition of gossip is used in its broader sense without any gender discrimination subtext:

(9) *You know, I mean, that gossip is absolutely …substantive in human nature. We're all constantly talking about each other and about what we think we know or heard or saw, overheard. And we use this sort of medium of exchange between us to enhance the human condition. It helps us figure out what we think. It helps us sort out our ideas morally. Do we approve when we're gossiping? Are we approving, or are we disapproving, or are we trying to figure out what we think? And that*

a lot of gossip is just this idea of, let me tell you a story (D. Bianculli. Remembering Syndicated Gossip Columnist Liz Smith).

To sum up, it appears that the gender dimension in the interpretation of *gossip* is rather important for the assessment of any metacommunicative situation. It helps to explicate the perlocutionary effect on the Hearer and to comprehend the Speaker's attitude towards the communicative situation which becomes a topic of his / her utterance. The pragma-semantic functioning of the lexeme *gossip* appears unstable, flexible and dependent on whether it is used in a female or a male discourse or in a neutral self-referential or social discourse with its general more abstract meaning. This fact is supported by the reasoning of Carston, who states that "there are pragmatic processes of meaning enrichment and adjustment which have no linguistic mandate but are wholly motivated by considerations of communicative relevance" (Carston, 2012: 2).

It is important to note that metacommunicative defamatory predicates usage in social discourse does not reflect the actual situation in the society, which concerns defamation. When we analyse a metacommunicative predicate such as *gossip (gossiping)*, we place emphasis upon the Speaker2's assessment of somebody's speech as *gossiping*. When we argue that the female discourse of gossip is predominantly assessed negatively, it means that the lexeme *gossip* is used by the Speaker2 to denote women's talk in a negative way, regardless of the content of the women's utterances: positive, neutral or negative. I did not conduct any quantitative analysis, but continuous sampling of utterances, containing a metacommunicative lexeme, namely *gossip*, gave two examples only, where the Speaker2 assessed males' talk, using this lexeme with an attribute possessing a negative connotation. These were the statements where the Speaker compared a man's behaviour with that of a woman.

It might sound self-contradictory, but according to data published in the journal Social Psychological and Personality Science in 2019 by researchers from the University of California (Berkley), namely Robbins and Karan, female gossip tends to be neutral and involves information-sharing. Female gossip appears to be less harmful than its male counterpart. They looked at data from 467 people—269 women and 198 men. In total, 4,003 instances of gossip were researched. Almost three-fourths of gossip was neutral. Negative gossip (604 instances) was twice as prevalent as positive (376) (Warren, 2019).

This contradiction between social discourse as a phenomenon and social discourse analysis from the linguistic perspective manifests the fact that there is a discrepancy between the Speaker meaning and the Hearer inference of a defamatory statement. It proves that there is a deflection of input information, when the Hearer passes it through his / her individual cognitive space. The Gender cognitive dimension becomes that vector of input information deflection, which stimulates the Hearer to subconsciously falsify data, attributing negative meaning to neutral talk.

3.3   Age Dimension of Cognitive Space

According to psychological evaluations (Nicholson, 2001; Robins & Karan, 2019; Warren, 2019, etc.), people are engaged in gossiping from almost their early childhood. The reason for this type of social activity is quite positive: they look out for each other. Unlike some negative forms of gossip, this type is categorized as "prosocial behaviour", which is intended to benefit other people. A child's gossip is aimed at warning others about potentially-bad individuals. Children tend to find a positive component in gossiping, such as promoting generosity, or relieving stress and preventing exploitation (Cueto, 2016).

My research proves the existing psychological standpoint that the notion of gossip appears to become rather complex for above-ten children. The concept formation in a child's mind starts with an individual, simplified idea of this phenomenon. The individual concepts[2] of gossip vary in their comprehension, from "revealing a secret" to "casting aspersions on; making a wrongful accusation"; the latter is closer to its proper meaning:

---

[2]It is termed after John McCarthy, who described individual and universal concepts using the example of "Mike's telephone number" in his article "First Order Theories of Individual Concepts and Propositions" (Stanford University, 2000).

(10) *"I have this friend that used to be so nice but she changed and started gossiping about me! She said that I like this guy …"* (Mia, 10 years old) (to gossip = to reveal a secret);

(11) *"Yes, I had 2 best friends: A girl and I had a crush on a boy… So she started gossiping about me and he chose her over me"* (Makeda, 10 years old) (to gossip = to cast aspersions on).

Children's discourse is much more emphatic than adults' discourse when it concerns gossip. Apparently, a child appears to be extremely sensitive to gossip, even much more than an adult in a similar discourse:

(12) *"I hate gossip. It hurts people and the person who is the subject of the rumor or gossiped about feels really bad about themselves"* (Shaunagh, 10 years old).

The word *hate*, when combined with the lexeme *gossip*, makes the whole utterance more emphatic, conveying an overall negative assessment of defamatory communication.

The emotional assessment of gossip tends to become more abstract and more neutral with ageing. An elder group of kids in their self-referential discourse can reduce the negative assessment component to its minimum:

(13) *"I cut my hair WAY SHORT and dressed more 'in style' and gossiped and flirted a lot. Then the guy I liked actually asked me out, but he didn't like the fact that I was all preppy so he dumped me the silent treatment way. Then I changed back to my normal self"* (Alicia, 12 years old).

The meaning of the verb *gossip* in an individual concept of a 12-year-old girl is equal to "talk a lot" or "chatter".

It is highly important that the pragmatic component of the meta-communicative utterance appears to balance between the age dimension and gender dimension and self-referential discourse. The assessment of gossip as "mean-spirited talk about others" becomes more neutral with ageing and is often classified as "harmless chatter", but simultaneously the gender dimension aggravates the negative assessment of gossip when female discourse is involved. On the contrary, self-referential discourse neutralizes the negative assessment of gossip in any age group—even in the youngest one.

Interestingly enough, the neutrality maximum of gossip assessment can be observed in the utterances regarding prominent figures. The lexeme is often used in word combination with a positive connotation, e.g. *good gossip*:

(14) *Franklin Roosevelt, from what I understand, always loved to be around people who liked to laugh, who liked to have fun. He loved having fun in many, many different ways. He enjoyed his cocktail hour. He loved good gossip (American Experience interview, 1999).*

The same pragmatic meaning is conveyed in "Current news for people in public media" by Bill Moyers, who talks about Lyndon B. Johnson and Wilbur Mills:

(15) *They gossiped for an hour or so, shared rumors about friends and enemies, relived old battles in Congress, schemed about bills then pending - and then LBJ began to press the flesh: what Washington called "The Treatment" (Wilbur Mills to LBJ: 'We ain't gonna give money to folks without some strings attached'; May 18, 2006).*

The perlocutionary effect of *gossip* corresponds to *small talk* in this context, representing neutrality of judgement.

Consequently, the cognitive space age dimension demonstrates the variability of pragmatic meaning of age-specific utterances. The utterances' perlocutionary effect on the Hearer reflects the degree of PCS negative assessment. This proves that the same defamatory metacommunicative lexeme can differ by its connotation and interpretative potential capacity while used in different age-specific discourses.

3.4   Structural Dimension of Cognitive Space: The Type of Observer

The perlocutionary effect of defamatory metacommunication depends also on an additional dimension, which can be termed the "structural dimension of cognitive space".

A significant role in the Speaker meaning assessment is played by the correlation of the Speaker's communicative role with the role of the Observer in metacommunication. We have already given the general description of the cognitive structure of metacommunication, but it makes sense to describe the role of the Observer, which greatly influences the pragmatic component of metacommunication.

The Observer in metacommunication is the person who witnesses the Precedent Communicative Situation (PCS) in which someone says something offensive to another person; for instance, John says to Tom: "What an idiot you are!" The Observer can also know about the PCS from hearsay. In any case, the defamatory utterance (or PCS as a whole) becomes the topic of the succeeding communication, or Current Communicative Situation (CCS), in which the Observer becomes the Speaker2 and estimates (or judges) the vocal act of the Speaker1 in the PCS. The Observer (the Speaker2) can say: "*John abused (offended, outraged, insulted, etc.) Tom*". This is communication about communication, or in other words, metacommunication.

The cognitive structure of metacommunication can differ due to the distribution of the communicative roles of its participants within both communicative situations. This distribution basically concerns the coincidence / non-coincidence of the roles of the Observer and the Hearer1, and the Speaker2, which defines the pragmatics of metacommunication and provides its cognitive structure dissimilarity on the strategic level. There can be several patterns, as follows:

Pattern 1. The role of the Observer coincides with the roles of the Hearer1 (= the Victim of abuse) and the Speaker2.

It means that John has called Tom an idiot and Tom is telling somebody about this fact. On the strategical level, Tom can choose different ways to pass this information along to his interlocutor. He can use a neutral verb, such as *call* (*John called me an idiot*). The communicative strategy of this choice will be as follows: the Speaker2 does not want to assess the communicative action of the Speaker1 and delegates this function to the Hearer. The reasons for this behaviour can be: (a) to give the Hearer2 the chance to estimate the PCS by himself / herself and to gain psychological support from the Hearer; (b) to elicit an emotional response from the Hearer which can be much more severe than it might have been if he had done it by himself; (c) to avoid negative assessment of the abusive communicative action by the Speaker1 so that he is not humiliated by complaints; etc. The Observer (or the Speaker2) can choose any metacommunicative predicate of defamation. What is important to note is that metacommunicative predicates do not only contain the elements of PCS assessment in their semantics and cognitive structure, but also specify the perlocutionary effect on the Speaker2. For instance, the cognitive structure of such defamatory predicates as *humiliate, abase, chagrin, chasten, shame, demean, mortify*, etc., contains components indicating what kind of effect the Speaker has on the Hearer, and what kinds of emotions are induced: feelings of *humility, humbleness, abjection*, etc. Sometimes the defamatory predicate semantic (and cognitive) structure is indicative of a specific perlocutionary effect. The verb *humiliate*, for example, points to such perlocutionary effect as *being ashamed or embarrassed*.

Pattern 2. The roles of the Observer and the Hearer1 (= the Victim of abuse) grow apart but the Observer's role coincides with the role of the Speaker2.

The Observer can act as a bystander of PCS (or the third party of the communicative situation) where someone has abused the other person, or he / she can speak from hearsay. In this case, the Observer is not a Victim of abuse. He / she speaks of the other person who has been abused by someone previously.

This situation supposes communicative turn-taking which is followed by turn-taking of communicative strategies of the participants. The estimation (or interpretation) of the CCS topic content (or its proposition) changes simultaneously: John abused me (it's a complaint) and *John abused Tom* (it's a critical judgement).

Strategically speaking, *a complaint* and *a critical judgement* accomplish different communicative functions. In case of a complaint, the Speaker2 basically relies on the Hearer's compassion. An enlarged context helps us disclose additional communicative strategies. The Observer can intend to explain the reasons for the precedent communicative failure or to discredit the Speaker1. In case of a critical judgement, the Observer2's intentions can vary greatly, from discrediting the Speaker1 to an ironical judgement of the entire communicative situation, or of the participants separately, their relationship or even the Victims of the PCS derision. The interpretation's accuracy is dependent on the accuracy and completeness of the cognitive space analysis or, in other words, the analysis of extralinguistic factors accompanying that communicative situation.

The Cognitive Space Structural Dimension analysis can also be important in case of semantic constraint. It is almost completely impossible to explain why some predicates cannot be used in certain communicative situations. In order to figure out a reason for this, we need to analyse the predicates' extralinguistic components and the participants' communicative roles distribution.

Pattern 3. The role of the Observer coincides with the roles of the Speaker1 and the Speaker2.

The role of the Observer can coincide with the roles of active participants of both communicative situations, i.e. their Speakers, but it happens very seldom due to the semantic constraint in the usage of defamatory predicates. For instance, it is almost impossible to say **I'm slandering…* or **I slandered…*, but it is not a completely semantic constraint; this constraint is derived from socially-prohibited activity. Being by its nature "*an utterance of false charges or misrepresentations which defame and damage another's reputation*" (Merriam-Webster Dictionary, 2019), slandering cannot become a topic of auto-referential discourse. I have found only two examples with the form *I slandered* in the Corpus of Contemporary American English (COCA). The first is an indirect speech utterance: (1) *Who says I slandered him.* The second is a self-referential utterance: (2) *Now I think that I slandered Bergen.* The latter was completed by the comment "*self-deprecation can be disarming against further criticism*" (MAG: Town and Country, February 2012). On their strategic level, the defamatory utterances of this type differ greatly: the first utterance can be interpreted as an accusation and the second utterance as a self-deprecation. The accusation is often aimed at the Speaker's intention to make the interlocutor apologize, while self-deprecation takes the form of the Speaker's apology for his / her hard-hitting action and usually intends to deprive the counterpart of the opportunity to judge his / her action this way.

For the same reason, we can seldom encounter a self-referential form of the verb with a reflexive pronoun. The following example is a rather rare case of such usage which demonstrates the Speaker's intention to rehabilitate himself or to prevent his interlocutors from delivering a negative assessment of his actions:

(16) *I humiliate myself by telling them I'd very much like to join the club and begging Krennup to untie me (G. Saunders. Bounty).*

The cognitive structure of the defamatory predicate *to offend* means it is highly unlikely that the said predicate will be used in the same auto-referential discourse, because it supposes the perlocutionary effect of *insult*, which demands the existence of the other actor of communication. Thus, a form of utterance such as *I offend (am offending, offended) myself* is not functional in social discourse practice.

It is also virtually impossible to say: *I am offending you here by saying...* because the state of offence is in the power of the Hearer perception. It is the Victim of defamation who can describe his / her own state as being offended, but not the Speaker. Even if it is possible to say so, it would mean intentional causation of offence, and verbalization of this communicative intention can be regarded as double offence, which contradicts the recommended rules of communication. This concerns the situation when PCS and CCS coincide in time (simultaneous metacommunication). If PCS has happened before, much earlier CCS (diachronous metacommunication), it sounds like an apology for the previous offensive utterance: *(17) I apologize if I offended you, Mrs. Stuart. It was not my intent (J. Dailey. The Proud and the Free)* or *(18) I'm sorry if I offended you earlier (P. Whitney. Until the End of Time)*. It is almost always accompanied by *I apologize* or *I'm sorry*.

This communicative role is also alien to the verbs *embarrass, chagrin, shame, discomfort* and others, for the same reason.

Thus, defamatory metacommunication patterns suppose a communicative strategic variety. This means that the same precedent communicative situation can be interpreted differently by different types of Observers. In other words, this variety is conditioned by proposition deflection through the individual cognitive spaces of the interlocutors in communication.

4   Conclusion

The analysis of defamatory communication and metacommunication via cognitive space dimensions suggests the attempt to present a new experimental pragma-semantic approach in cognitive linguistics and social discourse research. It supposes that the extralinguistic environment (or cognitive space), including the interlocutors (with their background and characteristic features), the communicative situation and the third party of communication (the Observer), determines how the Speaker and the Hearer meanings should be interpreted. Cognitive space dimensions serve as specific vectors of deflection of incoming and outcoming information. Thus, the same communicative information is perceived and comprehended differently by the participants of communication. While the semantics of the utterances remains relatively stable, the pragmatics varies greatly due to specificity of the interlocutors' cognitive spaces.

The quantity of the cognitive space dimensions and their specificity is not universal and conclusive. It depends on many factors of communication and the specificity of the lexical meaning of the word or word combination making up a body of the concept considered. This research has proved that the analysis of cognitive structure of lexemes is rather important for comprehension of the interlocutors' communicative strategies. The communicative strategies, in their turn, help to determine implicatures of the utterances, demonstrating how the Speaker and the Hearer meanings should be understood. The variability of the pragma-semantic meaning of the defamatory metacommunicative lexemes can be determined by looking at both intralinguistic and extralinguistic reasons which act as interdependent factors of communication. This approach can be used for the analysis of certain other language units and can reveal many new interesting facts connected with interpersonal communication.

References

Austin, John L. (1962). *How to Do Things with Words*. Clarendon, Oxford.

Babaitseva, V. V., & Maksimov, L. Y. (1987). *Sovremenny russkiy yazyik. Sintaksis. Punktuatsiya* (2nd ed.). Moscow: Prosvescheniye.

Bach, K. (2006). *The top 10 misconceptions about implicature*. [online] https://www.semanticscholar.org/paper/The-top-10-misconceptions-about-implicature-Bach/d093414bfbeb72a4e5932194677ea05b2215a207. Accessed 26 August 2020.

Bateson, G. (2002). *Mind and Nature*. Hampton Press. [online] https://www.personal.ceu.hu/corliss/CDST_Course_Site/Readings_old_2012_files/Bateson_MindNature.pdf. Accessed 7 July 2020.

Benking, H. (2019). *Cognitive Spaces*. ESCO Encyclopedia. [online] https://benking.de/systems/encyclopedia/newterms/. Accessed 7 July 2020.

Bennetts, L. The Real MacGraw. In: Corpus of Contemporary American English (COCA): MAG: Town and Country, February 2012. [online] https://www.english-corpora.org/coca/. Accessed 07 July 2020.

Carston, R., & Powell, G. (2004). *Relevance Theory—New directions and developments*. [online] https://www.academia.edu/13004828/Relevance_Theory_New_Directions_and_Developments. Accessed 26 October 2020.

Carston, R. (2002). *Thoughts and Utterances: The pragmatics of explicit communication*. Oxford: Blackwell. [online] https://www.academia.edu/4071393/Thoughts_and_Utterances_The_Pragmatics_of_Explicit_Communication_ROBYN_CARSTON_Thoughts_and_Utterances_For_Vlad_Thoughts_and_Utterances_The_Pragmatics_of_Explicit_Communication. Accessed 23 September 2020.

Carston, R. (2006). *Relevance Theory, Grice and the Neo-Griceans: A response to Laurence Horn's 'Current issues in Neo-Gricean pragmatics'*. [online] https://www.researchgate.net/publication/249939798_Relevance_Theory_Grice_and_the_neo-Griceans_A_response_to_Laurence_Horn%27s_Current_issues_in_neo-Gricean_pragmatics. Accessed 23 September 2020.

Carston, R. (2012). *Implicature and Explicature*. University College London. [online] https://www.researchgate.net/publication/265483734_Implicature_and_Explicature. Accessed 23 September 2020.

Coie, J., Terry, R., Lenox, K., Lochman, J., & Hyman, C. (1995). Childhood peer rejection and aggression as predictors of stable patterns of adolescent disorder. *Developmental Processes in Peer Relations and Psychopathology, 7*(4), 697–713. [online] https://www.cambridge.org/core/journals/development-and-psychopathology/article/childhood-peer-rejection-and-aggression-as-predictors-of-stable-patterns-of-adolescent-disorder/E269243897D9FE7E2750C23EC0DD6E73. Accessed 11 September 2020.

Cueto, E. (2016). *Children start gossiping at 5 years old, new study says, and that's probably actually a good thing*. [online] https://www.bustle.com/articles/158824-children-start-gossiping-at-5-years-old-new-study-says-and-thats-probably-actually-a-good. Accessed 26 August 2020.

Defamatory Communication Law and Legal Definition. (2019). [online] https://definitions.uslegal.com/d/defamatory-communication/. Accessed 23 September 2020.

Félix-Brasdefer, C. (2020). *Pragmatics at Indiana University*. [online] https://pragmatics.indiana.edu. Accessed 23 September 2020.

Grice, H. P. (1961). The causal theory of perception: Part I. *H. P. Grice—Proceedings of the Aristotelian Society, 121*, 121–152.

Grice, H. P. (1969). Utterer's meaning and intentions. *the Philosophical Review, 78*(2), 147–177.

Grice, H. P. (1975). Logic and conversation. In P. Cole & J. Morgan (Eds.), *Syntax and Semantics 3: Speech Acts* (pp. 41–58). New York: Academic Press.

Grof, S. (1964). Mind, nature and consciousness: Gregory Bateson and the new paradigm. *Journal of Transpersonal Psychology, 8*, 121–147. [online] https://web.archive.org/web/20111018103753/http://www.stanislavgrof.com/pdf/Gregory_Bateson.pdf. Accessed 17 September 2020.

Gurevich, L. S. (2009). *Kognitivnoye prostranstvo metacommunikatsii (Cognitive Space of Metacommunication)*. Irkutsk: IGLU.

Horn, L. R., & Ward, G. L. (2004). *Handbook of Pragmatics*. [online] https://www.scirp.org/reference/ReferencesPapers.aspx?ReferenceID=1093233.

Horn, L. (2006). Speaker and hearer in neo-Gricean pragmatics. *Wai Guo Yu/Journal of Foreign Languages, 164,* 2–26.

Kecskes, I., & Horn, L. R. (2007). *Explorations in pragmatics: Linguistic, cognitive and intercultural aspects.* Berlin: Walter de Gruyter GmbH & Co. KG. [online] https://www.researchgate.net/publication/332708009_Exp lorations_in_pragmatics_Linguistic_cognitive_and_intercultural_aspects. Accessed 9 September 2020.

Lenz, F. (1997). *Speaking of Speech Acts.* [online] https://webdoc.sub.gwdg.de/edoc/ia/eese/artic97/lenz/5_97.html. Accessed 21 October 2020.

Meadows, D. H., Meadows, D. L., Randers, J., & Behrens, W. W. (1972). *The Limits to growth.* Universe, New York [online] https://benking.de/systems/encyclopedia/newterms/. Accessed 7 July 2020.

Merriam-Webster Dictionary. (2019). [Online]: https://www.merriam-webster.com/dictionary/slander. Accessed 07 July 2020.

Morris, C. W. (1946). *Signs, language and behavior.* New York: Prentice-Hall. Reprinted, New York: George Braziller, 1955. Reprinted in Charles Morris, 1971, *Writings on the General Theory of Signs.* The Hague: Mouton.

Nicholson, N. (2001). The new word on gossip. *Psychology today* (May 1, 2001, last reviewed June 9, 2016). [online] https://www.psychologytoday.com/us/articles/200105/the-new-word-gossip.

O'Rourke, J. (2008). *The truth about confident presenting.* Prentice Hall. [online] https://www.cambridge.org/core/books/truth-about-confid ent-presenting/AE5A41D63A6383A4003029C175A55B8C. Accessed 09 September 2020.

Peverelli, J. P. (2000). *Cognitive Space: A social cognitive approach to Sino-Western cooperation.* Delft: Eburon.

Peirce, C. S. (1994). *Peirce on signs: Writings on semiotic* (J. Hoopes, Ed.). Chapel Hill: University of North Carolina Press.

Peirce, C. S. (1997). *Pragmatism as a principle and method of right thinking: The 1903 Harvard lectures on pragmatism by Charles Sanders Peirce* (Edited, Intro., and with a Commentary by Patricia Ann Turrisi). Albany: State University of New York Press. [online] https://philpapers.org/rec/PEIPAA. Accessed 23 September 2020.

Robbins, M. L., & Karan, A. (2019). Who gossips and how in everyday life? *Social Psychological and Personality Science.* [online] https://www.researchg ate.net/publication/332828074_Who_Gossips_and_How_in_Everyday_ Life. Accessed 21 October 2020.

Schlesinger, I. M. (1995). *Cognitive Space and linguistic case: Semantic and syntactic categories in English.* Cambridge: Cambridge University Press.

Online publication date: October 2009. [online] https://doi.org/10.1017/CBO9780511551321. Accessed 21 October 2020.

Searle, J. (1969). *Speech acts: An essay in the philosophy of language.* Cambridge: Cambridge University Press.

Sperber, D., & Wilson, D. (1985). Loose talk. *Proceedings of the Aristotelian Society, 86,* 153–171.

Sperber, D., & Wilson, D. (1995). *Relevance: Communication and cognition.* Oxford: Blackwell. [online] https://www.academia.edu/9257754/Dan_Sperber_and_Deirdre_Wilson_Relevance_Communication_and_Cognition_. Accessed 5 October 2020.

Sperber, D., & Wilson, D. (1998). The mapping between the mental and the public lexicon. In P. Carruthers & J. Boucher (Eds.), *Thought and language* (pp. 184–200). Cambridge: Cambridge University Press.

Sperber, D., & Wilson, D. (2002). *Pragmatics, modularity and mind-reading.* [online] https://www.dan.sperber.fr/wp-content/uploads/2002_wilson_pragmatics-modularity-and-mind-reading.pdf. Accessed 21 October 2020.

Turansky, I. I. (2006). *Semanticheskaya kategoriya intensivnosti v angliiskom yazyike.* Moscow: Vysshaya Shkola.

Wilson, D. (2003). *Relevance and lexical pragmatics.* [online] https://www.researchgate.net/publication/238625989_Relevance_and_Lexical_Pragmatics. Accessed 19 October 2020.

Wilson, D., & Sperber, D. (2004). Relevance Theory. In L. R. Horn & G. Ward (Eds.), *The Handbook of Pragmatics* (pp. 607–632). Malden, MA: Blackwell.

Warren, J. D. (2019, May 3). *UC Riverside study busts myths about gossip.* University of California, Riverside. [online] https://news.ucr.edu/articles/2019/05/03/uc-riverside-study-busts-myths-about-gossip. Accessed 21 October 2020.

Watzlawick, P. (1967). *Pragmatics of human communication (with Beavin and Jackson).* [online] https://www.geosoc.org/schools/adult/docs/prag1.html. Accessed 21 October 2020.

Exploiting Irrational Evaluations: The Discursive Features of Scams Across Genres

Patrizia Anesa, Ismael Arinas Pellón,
and Azianura Hani Shaari

1   The Language of Scams

Technological advances have inexorably paved the way for new forms of scams conducted on the Internet (Salu, 2004) and online scams constitute a dramatic risk for the victims both from a financial and an

---

Although this paper has been planned, written and reviewed jointly, responsibility for the different sections may be assigned as follows: Anesa is responsible for Sects. 1 and 3; Arinas Pellón is responsible for Sect. 4; Shaari is responsible for Sect. 2.1; Anesa and Arinas Pellón are responsible for Sects. 2.2 and 5; Anesa and Shaari are responsible for Sect. 6.

P. Anesa (✉)
Department of Foreign Languages, Literatures and Cultures, University of
Bergamo, Bergamo, Italy
e-mail: patrizia.anesa@unibg.it

I. Arinas Pellón
Departamento de Lingüística Aplicada C. T., Universidad Politécnica
de Madrid, Madrid, Spain
e-mail: ismael.arinas@upm.es

© The Author(s), under exclusive license to Springer Nature
Switzerland AG 2021
P. Anesa and A. Fragonara (eds.), *Discourse Processes between Reason
and Emotion*, Postdisciplinary Studies in Discourse,
https://doi.org/10.1007/978-3-030-70091-1_3

emotional perspective. This study investigates the main persuasion strategies which characterize different types of scams, and the two main types of online frauds investigated are "419" or "advance-fee fraud" (AFF) and "romance" scams. Typically, the advance-fee fraud is based on convincing the targets of the need or the opportunity to place money in an overseas account. The victim is offered a share in return for their collaboration with the transfer, but once the advanced payment is made by the victim, the promise never materializes. A similar fraud is represented by the online dating romance scam, in which scammers contact their targets via social networks or dating sites and subsequently manage to lure the victim into the belief that they are in a romantic relationship. When this objective has been achieved the victim complies with monetary requests with the illusion that it will consolidate an authentic love story.

Previous studies concerning online scams have focused on the persuasive techniques used by scammers in convincing and manipulating victims, and on how persuasive language skills can influence people's emotions (Jones et al., 2015) and cognitive behaviour (Modic & Lea, 2013). According to Cukier et al. (2007), among the most common persuasion techniques used by scammers, strategies can be found which trigger strong emotional reactions, which, in turn, challenge the victims' ability to think clearly.

The intelligence and level of education of the targets of scams should not be underestimated. For instance, victims include university professors, businesspeople, psychotherapists, and even congresspeople (see Kich, 2005: 13). Indeed, despite the manifest fraudulent nature of the texts, the persuasive strategies employed in scams render the warning signs invisible to the victims.

This chapter analyzes what type of discursive devices are employed to attract the victims' interest and subsequent trust, to the extent that they become unable to recognize the linguistic and discursive signs which

A. H. Shaari
Center for Research in Language and Linguistics, The National University of Malaysia, Bangi, Malaysia
e-mail: azianura@ukm.edu.my

represent distinct manifestations of a fraud. The underpinning consideration on which this analysis is based is that persuasion is a core aspect of human interaction, which can be used as a manipulative tool, as happens in the case of fraudsters (Ferreira, 2016: 29). In this respect, reason and emotion become two irreconcilable aspects of message processing and, in both types of fraud, scammers implement discursive devices which hinder the victims' ability to process the information rationally.

The hypothesis to be tested is that the two different types of scams draw considerably on similar communicative strategies, most notably the exploitation of errors of judgement. Our reading of errors of judgement is here indebted to Lea et al. (2009); more specifically, their taxonomy including motivational and cognitive judgement errors (2009: 25–34) is used to identify the persuasive processes adopted by the scammers in order to construct credible narratives.

This study draws on previous research on scam messages (see Anesa, 2020; Arinas Pellón et al., 2005) and aims to gain a finer understanding of how discursive strategies are employed for fraudulent purposes across genres. Moreover, the results obtained may prove useful for the definition of linguistic models which can be implemented in the detection of adversarial fraudulent strategies.

2　Research Framework

2.1　Communicative Model

The hyperpersonal model of computer-mediated communication (CMC) postulates that "users exploit the technological aspects of CMC in order to enhance the messages they construct to manage impressions and facilitate desired relationships" (Walther, 2007: 2538). This model lies within the concept of selective self-presentation which discusses the way online users employ social media and their unique features to achieve specific communication purposes. The most fascinating aspect of online communication, according to Walther et al. (2015), lies in its capacity to draw on some fundamental elements of interpersonal communication, by focusing on the most central and essential processes which take place in online communication experiences. Online relationships are developed and established through message-exchange processes in which texts and symbols work as the primary instruments of human virtual expression.

The model presents some of the mechanisms which make online communication an interesting platform for establishing the desired self-presentation. Firstly, online messages are modifiable. Unlike verbal communication, chat rooms in social networks, for instance, provide space for online users to edit messages before submitting them to receivers. In addition, online users, especially in asynchronous communication, have ample time to construct and refine their messages and, consequently, speech acts in virtual communication are predetermined and deliberate (Walther, 2007). Some senders adjust their linguistic behaviours (in online chats) after predicting receivers' future responses. Furthermore, senders do not have to project their natural body language and can hide their non-deliberate actions from receivers.

As a flexible and cross-disciplinary model, the hyperpersonal framework has been utilized by scholars from various research areas such as education, psychology and linguistics. Some studies have employed the model to understand users' behaviour (Tidwell & Walther, 2002) and identity (Walther et al., 2010) while others have analyzed senders' linguistic strategies in persuading targeted receivers (Annadorai et al., 2020). Previous researchers of the online dating romance scam have utilized this model to explore the way scammers exploit virtual communication platforms and make use of the interface attributes of social media to persuade victims by enhancing impressions using various persuasive strategies and social cognitive approaches. Annadorai et al. (2020) posit that scammers exploit online communication platforms by creating various assumed identities to convince and persuade victims. In particular, editable features provided on social media are used to create charismatic virtual images and desirable self-presentations, and the overwhelmingly positive impression that the victims are left with renders them emotionally vulnerable and open to exploitation (Annadorai et al., 2020).

Table 1 Result of standard deviation analysis on the number of words per document (AFSC)

Population standard deviation, σ	193.09594206011
Variance (population standard), σ^2	37286.042840081
Number of documents in corpus	507
Sum	150,883
Mean	297.59960552268
Standard error of the mean ($SE_{\bar{x}}$)	8.5841616771683 (± 8.6 in relation to mean)

2.2   Material

The corpus compiled consists of two subcorpora: one including romance scams (referred to as RSC) and one including advance-fee scams (AFSC). All the texts were collected between 2004 and 2018, and the language used is predominantly English.

The first corpus (RSC) consists of two sections: (a) templates used by the criminal organization led by Olayinka Ilumsa Sunmola,[1] and (b) 30 authentic conversations via chat and email collected predominantly in Malaysia between 2016 and 2018. The sets of online chats (from 30 victims) were selected using a purposive sampling technique. The sample was selected based on the following characteristics: (1) male or female online users who have experienced a romance scam; (2) victims who have made at least one financial transaction with the criminals; (3) victims who are willing to share their experience and data (online conversations with scammers) with the researchers.

The second corpus (AFSC) includes 507 emails referring to advance-fee frauds. More specifically, the AFSC may be characterized as follows:

- 151,820 tokens
- 8,039 types
- Shortest email in corpus: 9 tokens, 9 types
- Longest email in corpus: 1,388 tokens, 452 types (Table 1).

---

[1]Olayinka Ilumsa Sunmola, 32, of Lagos, Nigeria was the leader of a scamming organization based in South Africa which targeted female victims across the USA. On March 2, 2016, after two days of testimony at his criminal trial, he changed his plea from "not guilty" to "guilty" on all counts.

The email categories included in AFSC are as follows:

a. Over-invoice emails: the fraudster pretends to be a member of the public administration of an African country (usually Nigeria). This public servant states that some project has been over-invoiced and he, as a government officer, cannot take hold of the extra money. Thus, he suggests transferring the money to the victim, who can retain a percentage as compensation, and transferring the rest to another account (see example 1).

> (1) *"Following the ongoing settlement of the long awaited foreign contract debt, during our verification exercise, we came across an over-invoiced Contract."*[2]

b. Deposed leaders and asset transfers emails: these come from fictitious relatives or lawyers of deposed African dictators. The scammers state that they need help to transfer large amounts of money to a safe bank account in Europe, promising a sum as compensation. In the case of Asset Transfers, it is usually a victim of a dictator who needs help to conduct this type of operation (see example 2).

> (2) *"My name is Mr. Paul Chuba Harcourt, a nephew and adviser on Financial Exchange and Acquisition to the ousted President of Liberia His Excellency Charles Taylor. Following the current Rebel attack in my country, the Ex-President delegates me in respect to safekeeping of the money that arose through diamond sales to Europe, which I managed to leave the country with the sum of USD$12,000,000.00."*

c. The inheritance and dead foreigner scams: these represent two variations of the same narrative. In the former, a relative of a dead person offers to share the inheritance if the victim allows his/her bank account to be used for the transfer of several million US dollars. In the latter, a lawyer invites the victim to pose as the next of kin of one of his foreign clients who has died in a tragic accident. Acceptance will be rewarded with a substantial portion of the deceased client's money (see example 3).

---

[2]Any inaccuracy present in the corpus has been preserved in the examples cited.

(3) *"We would need you as a Foreigner acting as the next of kin and sole benefactor to the inheritance of Mrs. Ann Barbara Myers to forward a claim form to this Bank which am going to secure for you to claim this money into your bank account. The money will be paid to you for us to share in the ratio of 60% for me and 40% for you."*

d. Charity Gifts: a dying person offers a fortune only on the condition that the receiver donates part of it to charities (see example 4).

(4) *"At some point my business grossed over $40 million before I was forced to leave due to my health. I want to donate the money that is left in my business account to you because I want you to assist other people in need."*

e. Donation Plea emails: these involve a person who desperately needs to recover some money because he/she has been affected by war, natural disaster, or some legal injustice. Typically, the story can be verified via Internet links and attached documents (trial rulings, contracts, and links to online newspapers) (see example 5).

(5) *"I am Captain Roger Dan serving in U.S Military Base in Afghanistan, I have a total sum of $1.3 Million US dollars I wish to use the funds for investments that is why I seek for your assistance to be my partner."*

f. Lottery scams: these have the form of an official notification of a random prize from either a national lottery organization or a company lottery. Either in the email or upon receipt of the victim's reply, the scammers indicate that the victim has to advance an amount of money to a specific account to cover taxes and legal fees in order to receive a prize (see example 6).

(6) *"[…] we ran an online e-mail beta test which your email address won £950,000.00 (Nine Hundred And Fifty Thousand Great British Pounds Sterling). A winning cheque will be issued in your name by Google Promotion Award Team."*

3   Persuasive Dynamics

Online frauds are typically based on social engineering, intended as a process through which confidential information is obtained (cf. Lea et al., 2009: 18). For instance, in the case of the Lottery scams (see example 7), which are frequently used for identity theft purposes, these emails request personal details with the excuse of verifying the identity of the winner.

> (7) "[…] or processing and remmitance of your winnings, you are required to contact our designated claims agent with the following underlisted informations: FULLNAMES, CONTACT ADDRESS, COUNTRY, SEX, AGE, OCCUPATION, TELEPHONE NUMBER, NATIONALITY. Once again congratulations from our members of staff, Happy new year."

In AFSC, some of the characteristics which should be indicative of the false nature of such emails are the following:

a. The purpose is illegal (transfer of funds illegally obtained, embezzlement, assuming a false personality, providing money for bribes, forgery, etc.) (see example 8).

> (8) "We have resolved that you take 30% of the total amount for your assistance because it is impossible for us to claim the over-invoiced amount here in Nigeria without your assistance."

b. The proposal assures that everything is perfectly legal (see example 9).

> (9) "I will not fail to inform you that this transaction is 100% risk free and on smooth conclusion of this transaction, you will be entitled to 30% of the total sum as gratification, while 10% will be set aside to take care of expenses that may arise during the time of transfer and also telephone/fax bills, and 60% will be for me."

c. The person proposing the business is a relative/employee of highly questionable politicians. The circumstances described indicate that helping these people would mean cooperating in a scheme for the transfer of capital under judicial investigation (see example 10).

(10) *"I am Mrs. Jewel Howard Taylor, a wife of embattled President of war torn Liberia, Mr. Charles Taylor."*

d. The email insists on the need for secrecy and speed (which would be unnecessary if the procedure was legal) (see example 11).

(11) *"Please I would like you to keep this proposal as a top secret and delete it if you are not interested."*

e. Despite the secrecy of the business, the proponent is sending it to a stranger whose dependability has never been proved (see example 12).

(12) *"You may be quite surprised at my sudden contact to you but do not despair, I got your contact from a business site on the internet and following the information I gathered about you, [...]"*

f. If the scheme were true, the sender would risk losing several million US dollars to a stranger (see example 13).

(13) *"What we want from you is the accordant that you will let us have our own share when this fund ($31.5musd) finally gets into your account."*

g. These letters often contain several morpho-syntactic mistakes. Such inaccuracies are often intentional, aiming to create in the victims the illusion that the senders are uneducated and thus harmless individuals (see example 14).

(14) *"it has come to our notice that your Over payment of US$ 10.000.000.00 MILLION has being deposit to FEDERAL RESERVE BANK USA for further credit to your bank account as the original beneficiary."*

h. The messages are in plain text and the return addresses are free anonymous accounts (Tsow & Jakobsson, 2007: 13).

In romance scams similar indicators of a fraud are also present and include the following processes:

a. Profiles display an aura of perfection. In the case of male scammers, they are often wealthy people who live abroad and are very successful in their jobs. Typically, the scammer presents himself as a widower with one child, so as to generate sympathetic and compassionate feelings in the victim. In the corpus, several examples of this type of scenario may be found:

> (15) "I want to spend the remaining seconds of my life with my woman.
> I have a house in the States, I have one in Dubai
> [...]
> I am successful! I met Mary in Paris but again in the States and we got married. Till the very moment she left this world, she was every thing in my life"

b. Scammers try to move quickly to communication via email or instant messaging, while they persistently avoid face-to-face meetings.

> (16) "Drop a note/email address and I'll reply instantly. Just you may wish to email too, my email benjohnson6690 at G.M.A.I.L dot cum You on my mind."

c. Criminals express profound feelings of love a very short time after the beginning of the correspondence. Clichéd expressions and romantic words permeate their texts. Common expressions to refer to the victim include *angel*, *diamond*, *princess*, or *star*:

> (17) "You are sure the keeper of my star, wiper of my tears, carer of my soul, joy of my life, taker of my breath, reader of my mind, melter of my heart, lover of my world, reason for my living, hearer of my worries, bringer of my smiles, angel of my spirit, cover of my body, filler of all spaces, sweetest of souls."

d. Manipulation includes reflections about trust to make the victim feel compelled to reciprocate this feeling and comply with the scammer's request.

> (18) "You are my everything, and I love you more than life itself. I love you truly! I will be out of the door straight to the bank soon. I attached the copy of my check to this email and you already have my flight confirmation. Please remember this check is a secret I will never share with anyone else so please keep it to yourself."

Moreover, persuasive strategies used by romance scammers include: exaggeration of interest and sympathy towards the victim, offering interesting gifts and business proposals, convincing the victim to do as they say in addition to threatening the victims (Shaari et al., 2019).

Victims of both types of scams seem to be particularly influenced by the narrative strength of the story (Tsow & Jakobsson, 2007: 13) rather than its manifest inconsistencies. According to Tsow and Jakobsson (2007: 2), the persuasiveness of the scam narrative increases when it tells the readers something surprising, when it connects the message to well-publicized events, or when it informs the readers about an imminent change in their routine (see Table 2 for examples in AFSC).

The strategies adopted to create a powerful and credible narrative are in line with Tversky and Kahneman's (1981: 453) notion of framing intended as a technique used for influencing decision-making when facing a problem, from the point of view of behavioural economics. Indeed, decision-makers act differently according to the formulation of the problem, norms and habits, and their personal characteristics. Traditionally, the goal of the scams is to frame the emails as a riskless decision, which simply "concerns the acceptability of a transaction in which a

Table 2 Elements increasing narrative strength in scams (Tsow & Jakobsson, 2007)

Surprising event	Well publicized event	Changes in victim's routine
• You receive a prize in a lottery for which you never bought a ticket • You receive an inheritance from an unknown relative • You receive a donation from an unknown person • You are offered a conspicuous commission for transferring somebody's fortune to your bank account	• People mentioned in the email have appeared regularly in the news • The events mentioned in the email are linked to real references in online newspapers and on websites	• You are going to become a millionaire • You will become involved in business activities with famous politicians • You are asked directly for help from the victims of a natural or political catastrophe

good or service is exchanged for money or labor" (Kahneman & Tversky, 1984: 341).

In the case of romance scams, the accurate creation of a flawless romantic relationship, which is perfectly aligned to the needs and desires of the victims, contributes to hampering their ability to process messages rationally. Indeed, by idealizing the construct of love, the victim is unable to identify the signs of fraud that are manifest in the text. Generally, potential flaws in the stories are compensated by the overflows and excesses of the utterances used in the narrative especially when complimenting the victim and verbalizing emotional feelings. In this respect, the romantic narrative is punctuated with expressions of desire and commitment to a romantic relationship. As the scammers linger on details of their private life, a sense of trust and connection is established, and the rift between the imaginary narration and the implausibility of the promises made in the texts remains unnoticed. The money-love association is so strongly established that the concept of real love becomes irrevocably bound to the idea of helping a partner in need financially. The concrete element of money becomes inextricably linked to a series of undifferentiated concepts, such as love, trust, and belief.

In romance scams, the desire to believe in the relationship prevents the indicators of fraud from being perceived. With this type of fraud especially, a devastating conflation of feelings emerges. Victims do not want to accept the end of the relationship even when they realize that it is over and may be subsequently revictimized (Buchanan & Whitty, 2013; Whitty & Buchanan, 2012).

4   Cognitive Errors

Errors of judgement are astutely exploited by scammers in order to persuade the victims to comply with their requests, and such errors can be motivational and cognitive (Lea et al., 2009: 25–34). In particular, cognitive sources of errors may be categorized as follows:

- Norm activation: Some of the stories in the emails are interpreted by the victims as authentic, and they activate social norm responses, such as the norm to be helpful and to act as a good citizen. Health problems are often exploited as a means to activate pity and the desire to help and, consequently, to comply with the expected norm. Political problems may activate the civic responsibility of some victims; thus, words such as *asylum* (38 occurrences), *political asylum* (14 occurrences), or *refugee*[3] (22 occurrences) may trigger this type of social response among some email recipients.

- False consensus effect: Some stories imply that the scammer has selected the receiver specifically because they share some common characteristics (e.g. in the case of Charity Gifts, Donation Plea, Over-invoice, and Deposed Leader). Most emails give assurance that the email recipient has been selected by a computer system, but in Nigerian Letters the choice is explained as the result of some form of research (through relatives, business organizations, or the Internet) or using vague references to the need to contact a specific addressee. In these explanations, the qualities of honesty and trustworthiness may also be attributed to the receiver (e.g. 37 occurrences of *honest* and 24 occurrences of *trustworthy* are found).

- Authority: The mention of famous people (such as politicians or entrepreneurs), companies, or professionals working in the areas of law, banking, or the army seems to trigger a behavioural response, which is typically exploited in persuasive communication. The personalities cited in our corpus include: Jonas Savimbi, Mobutu Sese Seko, Stella Obasanjo, Sani Abacha, Charles Taylor, Jonas Kiyari, Laurent Kabila, Robert Mugabe, Saddam Hussein, Yasser Arafat, Bill Gates, and Queen Elizabeth II. Some of the companies mentioned are, for instance, Microsoft, Yahoo, Google, HSBC Bank, City Bank, and Central Bank of Nigeria. The reference to governments of African and European countries is also frequent, and so is the reference to departments of the public administration of these countries and the USA. The fact that the scam can be prototypically recognized as a legitimate genre (sales promotional letter or award notification) confers authority and credibility to the content of the email.

---

[3]On eight occasions the expression *asylum seeker* between parentheses appears as a clarification for the meaning of *refugee*.

- Altercasting: The scammer assumes a specific role and expects the prospective victim to act in the complementary role. For instance, if the scammer appears dependent, the victim acts as a protector; instead, if the scammer poses as a friend, the victim responds accordingly. The role of the dependent victim is the approach adopted in the case of the Deposed Leader, Charity Gifts, and Donation Plea plots, whereas the Over-invoice, Asset Transfers, Inheritance, and Dead Foreigner plots rely on the "friend" approach. A typical role assumed by the scammer is that of widow/widower or orphan. In this respect, the word *death* shows 105 occurrences in the corpus and is generally used in the context of stories arousing pity and requiring the assistance of the email recipient. The most relevant collocations of the word *death* are shown in Table 3.

These collocations indicate that the story develops around the idea of being lonely and having experienced the loss of a close relative. Another strategy focuses on the fact that the person needs help to fulfil his/her last wishes, using expressions such as *"I am not afraid of death hence I know where I am going"* (9 occurrences) or *"I know that after death I will be with Allah"* (1 occurrence).

Moreover, in 126 cases the scammers require *assistance*, which can be described as *personal, needed, kind, financial, special, good,* or *foreign.*

Table 3 Collocations of *death*

	Death	Other collocates
After + the +	death of my +	[husband/father] + I decided to [flee/move to]
Before his + (untimely) +	death +	we were + [religious affiliation]/my father had deposited with + [banking society]
Before the +	death of my +	[father/mother] + [simple past/present perfect]
Since his +	death +	I decided not to remarry or get a child/the family has been losing a lot of money

There are 31 examples where the scammers use the structure [conditional/other modal forms] + *assist me/us*. As regards posing as a friend, 41 of the scams begin with expressions such as *Dear Friend* (32), *My Dear Friend* (9 occurrences), *Dear kind hearted Friend* (1 occurrence), *Dear business friend* (1 occurrence), *Hello Friend* (7 occurrences), or *My Good Friend* (4 occurrences).

5   Exploiting Genre Awareness

Genre awareness is often employed by scammers to deceive their victims (see Arinas Pellón & Anesa, 2020). In particular, in the case of AFF the use of a genre structure which mirrors that of a genuine business proposal is particularly effective. For instance, focusing on a type of scam known as the Dutch Lottery scam (in CAFS 507), Table 4 presents a proposal for a rhetorical move structure of this type of fraudulent message, with examples of the language signalling those moves.

The order of the moves shows some degree of variation. Congratulations may be repeated at the beginning, in the middle, and at the end of the email, although this move is always present at the end of the notification. The move marked (*) presents several variants depending on the strategy followed. For example, some emails include a vague reference to the nature of the prize, such as *to contact and proceed with payment of your Lottery/contract/inheritance Funds.* Emails including this type of message are aimed at retargeting previous victims who may still be waiting to receive payment from a previous notification. The moves marked (**) are not always present; in the case of move (10), warnings against scammers and identity thieves are given, or pressure tactics are used, such as appealing to urgency or the consequences of a breach of confidentiality.

Schwartz et al. (2002: 1178) state that "modern behavioral economics has acknowledged that the assumption of complete information that characterizes rational choice theory is implausible." Along these lines, we can reason with Kahneman that "most judgments and most choices are made intuitively" and "the rules that govern intuition are generally similar to the rules of perception" (2003: 1450). Kahneman (2003: 1451) also aptly points out that reasoning is characterized by being

Table 4 Rhetorical moves for Dutch Lottery scams

Rhetorical moves	Language signalling the move
1. Sender's Full Address	[Different for each notification]
2. Subject of the Notification	Notification of Payment/Winning Notification/Award Notification
	Contact our claims processing officer (immediately)
3. Notification and Details of the Prize*	We are pleased to inform you of the + [announcement/the result of lottery winners]
	We wish to inform you that you
	This is to + (officially) + inform you + [that/of the release of]
	[all of these options are followed by the name of the lottery and the amount of the prize]
4. Explanation of Selection Process**	All participants were selected through a computer ballot system
	(All) participants for the draws were randomly selected and drawn from + [several Internet related options]
5. Mode of Payment	[includes instructions for contacting a claim officer]
	Remember, all prize money must be claimed not later than + [date]
6. Request for Contact and Details of Contact Person	To begin your claim, please contact your file/claim officer
	To begin your lottery claims, please contact your claims agent
7. Request for Personal Data	[Send/provide/forward] + the following information
8. Request of Fees and Taxes to Collect Prize**	and note that to procure your Approval Slip it would cost you + [amount of money]
	The only fee you have to pay is the courier company fee which is + [amount of money]
9. Congratulations and Farewell	Congratulations once again. Best regards

Rhetorical moves	Language signalling the move
10. Warnings and/or Pressure Tactics**	In order to avoid unnecessary delays and complications, please remember to quote your reference and batch numbers in every one of your correspondences with your agent. Furthermore, should there be any change of your address, do inform your claims agent as soon as possible You may also receive similar e-mails from people portraying to be other Organizations of yahoo Inc. This is solely to collect your personal information from you and lay claim over your winning. In event that you receive any e-mail similar to the notification letter that was sent to you, kindly delete it from your mailbox and give no further correspondence to such person or body

slow, serial, controlled, effortful, rule-governed, flexible, and neutral. Conversely, perception and intuition are fast, effortless, associative, slow-learning (need training to be effective), and emotional. When people make decisions based on impressions, they are reacting in an involuntary way because the intuitive thoughts come to their minds spontaneously. Judgements or rational thoughts, on the contrary, are explicit and intentional (Kahneman, 2003: 1452). As the overall capacity for mental effort is limited, any cognitive stimulus that is effortless, i.e. accessible, should trigger intuitive thinking. For example, the representation of categories by means of prototypes is highly accessible because "it allows new stimuli to be categorized efficiently, by comparing their features to those of category prototypes" (Kahneman, 2003: 1463).

Being faced with what may appear as a genuine business proposal (or, in the case of romance scams, as a genuine love message), victims are inclined not to process the message rationally. The similarity of the message to authentic texts of that type emerges not only in terms of the main rhetorical moves and steps, but also with regard to the general format and the visual presentation of the scams. Such texts display an increasing level of sophistication, which leads the targets to equate the seemingly authentic structure with the overall authenticity of the message received.

6   Conclusions and Further Applications

Both in romance scams and advance-fee scams the art of the scammer is to fabricate trust through discursive, linguistic and genre practices which can deceive the potential victims by diminishing their capacity to be alert to such strategies. Even though the types of frauds emerging in the two corpora are rather different, the strategies employed by scammers show significant resemblance. In both cases the victims are not the agents, but the pawns of a game, which is played entirely in the arena of a skilled organization of fraudsters. Both in romance and AFF scams a gap is created between the desire to believe the truthfulness of the story and the ability to process the information rationally. Once the victims are engaged in the fraudulent mechanism, they show a tendency to disregard the possibility that the text may not be genuine.

In particular, errors of judgement are employed in order to persuade the victims to comply with the scammers' requests. The main cognitive errors exploited are norm activation, false consensus effect, authority, and altercasting. These strategies limit the ability to process the message rationally and stimulate the visceral urge to comply with the fraudster's request.

Scammers also try to elicit an emotional rather than a logical way of processing messages. The technique includes a letter of appeal from someone who is dying of cancer or involved in a tragedy such as a war or a plane crash (Cukier et al., 2007). As Zuckoff (2005) states, cyber criminals manage to arouse empathy and romantic feelings which influence victims and make them believe that they are sharing similar situations, stories or even expectations with scammers.

Genre awareness is also shrewdly exploited by the scammers in order to defraud their victims. In the case of AFFs, scams follow the structural elements of business proposals, matching people's expectations. Similarly, in romance scams the scammers' profiles as well as the texts produced (be they chat messages or emails) tend to mimic genuine textual production. Although to those not involved the implausibility of the content may appear evident, the scammers manage to exploit the desire of the victims to believe in the message being read, which reduces their ability to process the message sensibly and judiciously.

Given the constant increase in the number of scams at a global level and the high degree of complexity that scamming processes have now reached, further research on this topic is undoubtedly needed. In particular, the future work of our team on this topic is also directed at leveraging data from this paradigm to develop an application[4] which is aimed at detecting the potential danger of business and romance scams. Consequently, it can contribute to the development of systems capable of neutralizing these messages.

---

[4]We are particularly indebted to Arvind Indal Chavhan (FTSM, UKM) for the great contribution offered to the development of the application. On a technical note, the classification algorithm employed is Random Forest and the coding language used is Python. NLKT (Natural Language Toolkit) is the suite of libraries employed to process language related data.

This application works as an alarm system that triggers real-time notifications and alerts users when communicating online. It involves a computational model that allows an online system to crawl data on the users' mobile phones or computers, through social media or other online communication networks. Using the data, the system will identify certain lexical features and items (driven from the corpus), to predict whether the online message is fraudulent or legitimate. As conversations continue, the software will match present online conversations with the existing database and provide alerts based on the percentage of similarities of language with the strategies, features and patterns of scam language.

As regards the future applications deriving from this project, it is also envisaged that the data obtained will be used for the creation of guidelines to be circulated, especially on sensitive sites, to raise awareness of fraudulent practices.

References

Anesa, P. (2020). Lovextortion: Persuasion strategies in romance cybercrime. *Discourse, Context and Media, 35,* 1–8.

Annadorai, K., Shaari, A. H., Kamaluddin, M. R., & Krish, P. (2020). Factors contributing to online dating romance scam victimization: A qualitative study. *International Journal of Psychosocial Rehabilitation, 24*(4), 4434–4447.

Arinas Pellón, I., & Anesa, P. (2020). Advance-fee scams: A corpus and genre analysis. In M. Fuster-Márquez, C. Gregori-Signes, & J. Santaemilia Ruiz (Eds.), *Multiperspectives in analysis and corpus design* (pp. 1–14). Granada: Editorial Comares.

Arinas Pellón, I., Gozalo Sáinz, M. J., & González González, T. (2005). Nigerian letters, Dutch Lottery and teaching an ESP genre. In L. Sierra & E. Hernández (Eds.), *Lenguas para fines específicos (VIII) Investigación y enseñanza* (pp. 89–96). Alcalá de Henares: Universidad de Alcalá de Henares.

Buchanan, T., & Whitty, M. T. (2013). The online dating romance scam: Causes and consequences of victimhood. *Psychology, Crime & Law, 20*(3), 261–283.

Cukier, W. L., Nesselroth, E. J., & Cody, S. (2007). Genre, narrative and the "Nigerian Letter" in electronic mail. *Proceedings of the 40th Hawaii International Conference on System Sciences 2007.*

Ferreira, A. (2016). Persuasion in scams. In M. Jakobsson (Ed.), *Understanding social engineering based scams* (pp. 29–47). New York: Springer-Verlag.

Jones, H., Towse, J., & Race, N. (2015). Susceptibility to email fraud: A review of psychological perspectives, data-collection methods, and ethical considerations. *International Journal of Cyber Behavior, Psychology and Learning, 5*(3), 13–29.

Kahneman, D. (2003). Maps of bounded rationality: Psychology for behavioral economics. *American Economic Review, 93*(5), 1449–1475.

Kahneman, D., & Tversky, A. (1984). Choices, values, and frames. *American Psychologist, 39*(4), 341–350.

Kich, M. (2005). A rhetorical analysis of fund-transfer-scam solicitations. *Cercles,* 14 [online]. http://www.cercles.com/n14/kich.pdf. Accessed 31 July 2019.

Lea, S., Fischer, P., & Evans, K. (2009). *The psychology of scams: Provoking and committing errors of judgment.* Exeter: Office of Fair Trading.

Modic, D., & Lea, S.E.G. (2013). Scam compliance and the psychology of persuasion. *Social Science Research Network* [online]. http://dx.doi.org/10.2139/ssrn.2364464. Accessed 10 October 2019.

Salu, A. O. (2004). Online crimes and advance fee fraud in Nigeria: Are available legal remedies adequate? *Journal of Money Laundering Control, 8*(2), 159–167.

Schwartz, B., Ward, A., Monterosso, J., Lyubomirsky, S., White, K., & Lehman, D. R. (2002). Maximizing versus satisficing: Happiness is a matter of choice. *Journal of Personality and Social Psychology, 83*(5), 1178–1197.

Shaari, A. H., Kamaluddin, M. R., Paizi, W. F., & Mohd, M. (2019). Online-dating romance scam in Malaysia: An analysis of online conversations between scammers and victims. *GEMA Online Journal of Language Studies, 19*(1), 97–115.

Tidwell, L. C., & Walther, J. B. (2002). Computer-mediated communication effects on disclosure, impressions, and interpersonal evaluations: Getting to know one another a bit at a time. *Human Communication Research, 28,* 317–348.

Tsow, A., & Jakobsson, M. (2007). *Deceit and deception: A large scale user study of phishing* [online]. https://www.cs.indiana.edu/pub/techreports/TR649.pdf. Accessed 1 August 2019.

Tversky, A., & Kahneman, D. (1981). The framing of decisions and the psychology of choice. *Science, 211*(4481), 453–458.

Walther, I. (2007). Ecological perspectives on language and literacy: Implications for foreign language instruction at the collegiate level. *ADFL Bulletin, 38*(3), 6–14.

Walther, J. B., DeAndrea, D., Kim, J., & Anthony, J. (2010). The influence of online comments on perceptions of anti-marijuana public service announcements on YouTube. *Human Communication Research, 36,* 469–492.

Walther, J. B., Van Der Heide, B., Ramirez, A., Burgoon, J. K., & Peña, J. (2015). Interpersonal and hyperpersonal dimensions of computer-mediated communication. In S. S. Sundar (Ed.), *The handbook of the psychology of communication technology* (Vol. 1, pp. 3–22). Malden, MA: Wiley Blackwell.

Whitty, M. T., & Buchanan, T. (2012). The online romance scam: A serious cybercrime. *Cyberpsychology, Behavior, and Social Networking, 15*(3), 181–183.

Zuckoff, M. (2005). Annals of crime: The perfect mark. *The New Yorker, 82*(13), 36–42.

The Rhetoric of Resistance: Women Regaining Power Through Language

Claire-Anne Ferrière

1   Introduction

If power dynamics are evident in discourse practices, it seems that in the case of the imbalanced power relations between men and women, power dynamics make it more difficult for women to speak out. This is what happened in the Harvey Weinstein case: Harvey Weinstein (now HW), the Hollywood mogul, allegedly abused dozens of women, and because of the unequal power relation between them, most of them kept silent about this for years, some even for decades. The mere act of speaking up publicly—as many women have been doing since October 2017—is therefore in itself an important discursive act that challenges established power dynamics. This ignited a movement that put women's voices at the forefront of the national stage: the movement rapidly expanded further than the HW case and turned into a national debate about

C.-A. Ferrière (✉)
Faculty of Languages, Lyon 3 University, Lyon, France
e-mail: claire-anne.ferriere1@univ-lyon3.fr

© The Author(s), under exclusive license to Springer Nature
Switzerland AG 2021
P. Anesa and A. Fragonara (eds.), *Discourse Processes between Reason and Emotion*, Postdisciplinary Studies in Discourse,
https://doi.org/10.1007/978-3-030-70091-1_4

women's rights and women's place in society. This features a shift from the personal to the political as theorized by Carol Hanisch in 1969: "One of the first things we discover in these groups[1] is that personal problems are political problems", or in other words "Women are messed over, not messed up!" (Hanisch, 1969). This movement protesting against women's status and oppression in society therefore sparked from personal experiences and from the recognition of commonality in those individual experiences, which calls to something more systemic, social. A shift from the personal to the political, in Hanisch's understanding of the term, is thus at stake in the development of the movement born from the Weinstein case. Women engage in a social struggle in order to protest against the situation: "Power relations are not reducible to class relations. There are power relations between social groupings in institutions and there are power relations between men and women, between ethnic groupings, between young and old, which are not specific to particular institutions. [...] Power relations are always relations of *struggle*, using the term in a technical sense to refer to the process whereby social groupings with different interests engage with one another. [...] Social struggle may be more or less intense and may appear in more or less overt forms, but all social developments, in any exercise of power, take place under conditions of social struggle. This applies also to language: language is both a site of and a stake in (class) struggle, and those who exercise power through language must constantly be involved in struggle with others to defend (or lose) their position" (Fairclough, 1989: 34–35; his emphasis). This overt struggle for power predominantly takes place through language. Indeed, it is through language—through written or oral accusations—that women in Hollywood shared their personal experiences in the hands of HW and thus denounce a system of abuse. It is also through language—through speeches—that speakers at the Second Women's March (now 2WM) stirred up the crowd. It is therefore essential to analyse the discourse practices by which women try and regain power—to study the "how"—the linguistic aspect—as much as

---

[1]Hanisch here refers to consciousness-raising groups which developed in the 1960s and in which women were and are still encouraged to share their personal experiences in an attempt to recognize that their experience of oppression is not unique and isolated but is actually shared by many other women.

the "what"—the sociological aspect. In particular, it will be interesting to study whether this shift from the personal to the political also figures in discourse and how. As a matter of fact, since women are challenging existing power relations and existing discourses and ideology,[2] and are thus disruptive, they need to convince their audience—the American people—that the struggle they are entering into is legitimate and that there are grounds for this social struggle: studying rhetoric, or how these women try to persuade their audience of the legitimacy of their claims, is thus a prerequisite to understanding the construction of the counter-discourse. This will therefore lead us to consider and analyse the rhetorical and pragmatic tools women in the new feminist move-ment use in order to put forward a common, alternative narrative about gendered power relations and convince their audience of the legitimacy of their claims, in particular in relation to authority and ideology. Partic-ular attention will be paid to how the different discourses intertwine and are related to one another in the building of this counter-discourse.

2   Ideology, Power, and Persuasion

It is taken for granted in this article that language and power are closely linked, all through the interplay of ideology. This is posited by Crit-ical Discourse Analysis (now CDA), a theory of and a methodology to analyse language according to which language is socially determined and determinant. It is a social act, shaped by social dynamics, considerations, and norms. It is not independent from society, but is an integral part of it, and as such is influenced by it. Society, the way it is structured, as well as social dynamics—dynamics between different social groupings—shape social practices, including social interactions and language. In that sense, language is not an individual production, but a social construct. Of course, individual speakers have some degree of freedom when commu-nicating, but CDA seeks to highlight the (social) frames into which interactions take place. This means that language is determined by non-linguistic, social elements: in that respect, CDA considers that language

---

[2]The notion of "ideology" will be defined in the section 'Ideology, power, and persuasion.'

is socially determined. Language is thus a "social practice" (Fairclough, 1989: 22) and as such is, like any other social practice, a form of social struggle. Power struggle in society is performed in two ways, either overtly, through force such as in dictatorships, or covertly, through ideology: "An ideology is a coherent set of ideas and beliefs adhered to by a group of people that provides an organised and systematic representation of the world about which they can agree" (Charteris-Black, 2011: 21–22). Ideology brings forth and justifies a social order in which the dominant groups are and remain in power. Language is essential in enforcing ideology: "One of the causal effects of texts which has been of major concern for critical discourse analysis is ideological effects – the effects of texts in inculcating and sustaining or changing ideologies" (Fairclough, 2010: 9). CDA therefore considers language to be one of the tools through which dominant groups convey their ideology: "scholars researching the interconnections between language and ideology build from the premise that patterns of discourse are framed in a web of beliefs, opinions and interests. A text's linguistic structure functions, as discourse, to privilege certain ideological positions while downplaying others – such that the linguistic choices encoded in this or that text can be shown to correlate with the ideological orientation of the text" (Simpson, Mayer, & Statham, 2010: 5). Dominant groupings control the social frame of language and discourse, and it is particularly important to keep in mind that not all individuals, especially individuals from minority groups (in terms of social minorities, not sheer numbers), have equal access to discourse, be it because they do not have access to the social contexts in which they can learn the codes or in which they can use it, or be it because their voices are not valued the same as the dominant group's. They are linguistically and socially invisible because they do not have access to mainstream discourse, the one that disseminates and justifies the dominant ideology. CDA therefore seeks to be "critical" of discourse and, more specifically, to highlight its social aspect and its dialectical link with social power: in other words, it seeks to call attention to the "role of discourse as a controlling force in society" and to "the way in which language is used to persuade and manipulate both individuals and social groups" (Bloor & Bloor, 2007: 1). Nevertheless, if language is a tool of oppression in social struggle and oppression, it is also a tool of social resistance: language is a tool to challenge existing ideology and to "change social relations of power" (Fairclough, 1989: 1). If language is a vector of ideology, it can also be a vector of social change.

Rhetoric is essential in covertly attempting to convey or challenge ideology. Rhetoric has been defined as the art of persuasion by Aristotle (Rapp, 2010), who identified three aspects in speech upon which rhetoric rests: the speaker, the subject of the discussion, and the listener, the audience. There are three corresponding means of persuasion according to which elements of communication are played upon. One of the means of persuasion thus rests on the character of the speaker, on whether or not they are deemed reliable, what is known as *ethos*. The speaker therefore has to show, through speech, that they are well-intentioned and knowledgeable and that the audience can trust them. Rhetoricians can also work on the audience's emotions in order to convince them, through *pathos*, arousing specific feelings into the audience because "emotions have the power to modify our judgements" (Rapp, 2010). The purpose is thus for speakers to arouse empathy in the audience to lead them to side with them, notably through story-telling, the recounting of some experience. Lastly, the speaker can base their rhetoric on the argument itself, *logos*, by demonstrating, through logic and proof, that what they are saying is true. Importantly for our purpose, this definition of rhetoric takes into account both the act of production and reception of language, an aspect CDA highlights as well for all language production—not only for persuasive acts of speech. For CDA, language is dynamic: it is a process, not a product. When studying language, the CDA analyst must take into consideration not only the text as a product, but the whole process of language production and also of language interpretation, which is inherent to the process. It is dynamic and dialectical: if language is shaped   and in some regards constrained—by ideology, it also perpetuates it, through its very use. CDA thus endeavours to study "discourse" rather than "texts", i.e. the whole process of production and interpretation of language imbued with ideology rather than texts as products, in order to draw attention to the "role of discourse as a controlling force in society" (Bloor & Bloor, 2007: 1).

This movement initiated by the HW case can indeed be defined as a power and ideological struggle, one that is achieved mainly through language: through language, women try and deconstruct the discourses that put them at a disadvantaged position in society. As such, discourses in this movement can be considered ideological and persuasive and one therefore needs to analyse the ideological effects and rhetorical means—*pathos, ethos, logos*—used by the women to persuade of the legitimacy of the ideological struggle they are entering into. In other words, how are rhetorical devices used in the texts to enact ideological struggle through discourse?

3   Corpus Justification and Methodology

In order to analyse the ideological struggle at stake in this movement, two sets of discourses were taken up for analysis in the corpus. The first sub-corpus is constituted of seventy accusations made against HW, spread across fifty-one texts and composed of 81,419 words. By speaking up, women entered into the ideological struggle through the recounting of personal experiences, which they denounce. Only accusations which were made public as part of the HW case after the publication of the article by Twohey and Kantor (Kantor & Twohey, 2017) on 5 October 2017 were included; some of the women accusing the movie mogul had already spoken out, more or less publicly, but those accusations were not taken into account since they did not participate in the building of the movement per se. Therefore, only the first public accusations done in the context of this scandal were included in the corpus. Some other women did not speak up publicly about what they went through but laid official complaints; those were not included either since they did not participate in the building of a counter-discourse against the movie mogul. Accusations that were made after 20 January 2018 were not included either. Indeed, the purpose of this analysis is to study the transition from the personal HW case into the more political social movement that the 2WM signals. It is nevertheless true that the majority of accusations against HW were made in the first month of the movement—sixty-one of the accusations were made public in October 2017—and if all the accusations whenever they were made can be considered to participate in the building of the movement, the 2WM necessarily rests upon those accusations that had already been made at the time, hence the decision to exclude those made afterwards for the purpose of this analysis. If these accusations published after the 2WM are important on a broader scale in the movement, they are not to be analysed from our—somewhat more reduced—transitional perspective.

The second set of discourses is composed of speeches delivered during the 2WM of 20 January 2018. This stage figures the shift from the personal to the political in the ideological struggle. If the WM is a national event during which numerous marches are being held across the country every year since 2017, only speeches from the Los Angeles 2018 WM were included in the corpus, cumulating in 32 speeches and 17,942 words. Los Angeles was the largest march and the sub-corpus was thus constituted with speeches from this event. The sub-corpus was assembled from different accounts of the event, but no official line-up could be found to ensure that all the speeches delivered during that day were included. At least two speeches—that of Sarah Hyland and Scott Adams—were identified but could not be recovered.

The corpus as a whole (WC) is composed of 99,361 words and spans from 5 October 2017 to 20 January 2018. It covers two sub-corpora and comprises different types of discourses—accusations, demands, politically-oriented speeches—with slightly different target audiences; if these differences were taken into consideration, the purpose of the analysis was to identify the common traits they share in order to confirm the working hypothesis that all the different texts actually work together in posing and constructing a counter-discourse and an ideological challenge to the established discourse and ideology. Therefore, the choice was made to study them both separately, to better identify the common features, and as a whole, to identify the characteristic of that counter-discourse that is being built through these different texts.

Both sub-corpora and the WC were analysed with Wmatrix, a software tool which enables a *data-driven* approach to the corpus through statistical profiling (frequency-sorted word lists and concordance lines) (Rayson, 2002). The computer-generated results guide the researcher in their analysis of their corpus. Concordance lines "presen[t] instances of a word or phrase usually in the centre, with words that come before and after it to the left and right" (Rayson, 2002: 4) and identify frequent segments rather than only words. Frequency-sorted word lists identify "the most commonly occurring words in the text" (Rayson, 2002: 4). It is also possible to compare the frequency of occurrence of words in the corpus with a reference corpus, the American English corpus provided by Wmatrix in our case (AmE06). It allows researchers to determine the words that are more salient in the corpus under study than in the reference corpus and thus to identify noteworthy features of the corpus. There are several tests to identify significant features of texts; one of them is log-likelihood (now LL). LL determines the probability of a significant difference in frequency between two corpora. LL scores over 6.63 and 10.82 "equate to there being, respectively, a 99 per cent and 99.9 per cent probability that the results are significant and not due to chance" (McIntyre & Walker, 2019: 158). Another tool that can be used to complement LL is the "log ratio" (now LR): it measures the size of the difference between the corpus under study and the reference corpus. For example, a LR of 1 indicates that an item occurs twice as much in one corpus than in the other. In other words, the frequency of occurrence of such a word in the corpus under study is significantly higher than in the reference corpus and is thus definitory of the corpus under study.

Both relative and compared word frequencies are interesting tools to analyse a corpus for different reasons: relative word frequency highlights the most prominent words in a corpus, identifying major linguistic trends, while compared word frequency pinpoints those features which make the corpus distinctive compared to a reference corpus. Both need to be taken into consideration in order to provide the most exhaustive analysis. Indeed, the article *the* can have a very high relative frequency, yet it does not mean it is a distinctive feature of a corpus since it is also very frequent in the English language in general and thus in a reference corpus. However, pronouns, determiners, conjunctions—typically grammatical words—should not be overlooked in a corpus either on the grounds that they tend to be very present in a reference corpus: personal pronouns play an important role in the corpus under study for example, as is demonstrated by LL and LR tests. Moreover, studying the relative word frequencies in a given corpus, in particular of lexical words, is also relevant since they nevertheless testify to some repetitions and some patterns that are interesting to analyse.

One last tool that was used to analyse the corpus is "semantic tagging". Lemmas—i.e. the basic, canonical forms of words—are classified and gathered into different semantic categories. These categories are then ordered according to their frequency in the corpus. It thus goes one step further than word frequency since different words categorized together through their meanings will score higher. New features can come to light. Semantic tagging can also be relative or be compared to an American corpus, again using the LL and LR scores to determine significant differences.

Software analysis highlighted some salient linguistic features of the corpus. This quantitative analysis was complemented with a more qualitative one, based on the "procedure for critical discourse analysis" provided by Fairclough (1989). This procedure is a set of 10 questions to guide the researcher in describing, interpreting, and analysing texts. They were thus used as a frame to identify the rhetorical and pragmatic means by which women claim back authority in order to convince the American people of the legitimacy of this ideological struggle they are entering into, and several of the elements described by Fairclough will be mentioned in this paper. Before presenting the results of those quantitative and qualitative analyses, it is important to say a few words on the link between ideology and power and on the significance of persuasion in establishing domination. This will then lead us to consider the linguistic evidence of the struggle for authority and the struggle for ideology that is at stake in the movement and in the discourse that supports it.

4   Analysis and Results

In order to enter into an ideological struggle, women first needed to enter a struggle for authority. Imbalanced power dynamics, in particular in the case of HW who was considered a well-respected man, mean that the women who spoke out needed to have their narratives legitimized: they needed to appear reliable in order for their stories to be believed. Only then could the ideological struggle they were entering into be accepted as legitimate and be supported, and only then could their authority as leaders asking for change be recognized. Rhetoric plays an important role in this process: first, through the building of a sense of community of shared experience and then through the building of a community of social action.

4.1   Struggle for Authority

The women who started speaking up with the HW case were silent/silenced up until that moment. They either did not dare to speak up about what they went through, or, if they did, they were not listened to. They therefore needed to establish their legitimacy now that they are speaking up because the accepted narrative was not one in which women fall prey to men abusing their power position. It is essential for them to have their narratives accepted as true.

4.1.1   Asserting Women's Authority as Truth-Tellers

Women's voices are often doubted in cases of sexual accusations (Epstein & Goodman, 2018), all the more so since there is a discrepancy in status between the accusers (the women) and the accused (here, Harvey Weinstein), which, according to Boltanski, Darré, and Schiltz (1984), can be suspicious: HW was a very powerful man in Hollywood—with a more elevated status than the women accusing him—and he was also known to be a philanthropist championing women's cause, among other things. This means that "le dénonciateur doit instituer une croyance et, au moyen d'une rhétorique, convaincre d'autres personnes, les associer à sa protestation, les mobiliser et pour cela non seulement les assurer qu'il dit vrai, mais aussi que cette vérité est bonne à dire et que la violence consécutive au dévoilement est à la mesure de l'injustice dénoncée"[3] (Boltanski et al., 1984: 3). Women in this case must therefore prove that their denunciation is disinterested and that they have nothing personal

---

[3]"The whistle-blower must establish a narrative and, through rhetoric, convince other people, lead them to unite with their accusation, rally them; in order to do that, they must prove that what they say is true, but also that this truth is worth telling, and that the violence that will result from the act of accusation is commensurate with the injustice that is denounced."

to gain in accusing HW. In order for their claims to be accepted as legitimate, women need to be accepted as being reliable: it is as much about what they are saying as how they are saying it.

In HW accusations, declarative sentences are used, in which agency is very clear: they are resisting the tendency to use the passive voice as is often the case in reports of sexual assault (Bohner, 2002). They precisely identify the participants and their role; in particular, they are not shying away from laying the blame on the person they consider is their aggressor: Harvey Weinstein. As a matter of fact, his name is mentioned 873 times in the first sub-corpus and the semantic category "personal names" is the 5th most represented category in the corpus: roles and participants are thus precisely identified. They adopt a decisive stance, leaving no place to doubt about what happened:

> We went to his office and we had a great conversation about his current film and the film that I was pitching. He seemed genuinely interested and I was excited. After about 30 minutes, he asked to excuse himself and go to the bathroom. He returned in nothing but a robe, with the front open, and he was butt naked. He told me to keep talking about my film and that he was going to hop into his hot tub that was adjacent to the room, just steps away. When I finished my pitch, I was obviously nervous, and he just kept asking to watch him masturbate. I told him I was leaving. He quickly got out of the tub, grabbed my forearm as I was trying to grab my purse, and he led me to his bathroom, pleading that I just watch him masturbate. My heart was racing, I was very scared. I pulled my arm away finally and headed to the door. He started following me and telling me that he could introduce me to Bob Weinstein and that I could get a three-picture deal, and that he would green-light my script. But I had to watch him masturbate. I was on the verge of tears, but I pulled it together and quickly exited. (Louisette Geiss, in Allred, 2017a).

It cannot be omitted that all the accusations were not spontaneous: press conferences were scripted and rehearsed, newspaper articles were proofread and formatted, and even accusations on personal social media could be carefully thought for before being published. Nevertheless, the important element here is the reception of, and the effect on, the audience. The accusations appear authoritative and the actions of each participant are described successively and chronologically: we can easily see the scenes unfold before our eyes. Tenses in particular are relevant in that respect: when recounting their experiences, they tend to use the simple past tense:

> Once we <u>were</u> alone, the mood immediately <u>changed</u>. He <u>behaved</u> inappropriately and <u>propositioned</u> a 'personal' relationship to further my career. (Anderson, 2017)

> He <u>called</u> me into his office and <u>told</u> me to sit on the couch. He then <u>sat</u> down next to me and <u>proceeded</u> to tell me how things <u>worked</u> in Hollywood. He <u>asked</u> me if I <u>was</u> good. I <u>started</u> to tell him about my training, and my acting experience, and he <u>said</u> 'No, I need to know if you're good.' (Heather Kerr, in Allred 2017b)

The use of simple tenses is one of the features identified by Fairclough as constituting categorical modality: "The prevalence of categorical modalities supports a view of the world as transparent – as if it signalled its own meaning to any observer, without the need for interpretation and representation" (Fairclough, 1989: 129). Similarly, there are barely any epistemic modals expressing doubt, such as *could*, *may*, etc., in the HW accusations.

Their accusations are also very detailed and precise: women give dates and places, specify events at which the encounters took place, and mention witnesses: "I was first introduced to HW at <u>the European premier of The Aviator in 2004</u>. I then ran into him again at <u>the Cannes film festival in 2006</u>" (Mimi Haleyi, in Allred, 2017c). Their stories can be corroborated, and they often are in third-person accusations which are made in newspapers: journalists checked the women's testimonies and tell their audience so, lending more credits to the women's words. They are providing as much proof as possible about what they are recounting in order to support their argument and appear credible and legitimate. They thus appeal to reason and logic (*logos*) as a necessary step to be recognized as victims who are legitimate in denouncing a system of abuse and in demanding changes. This is evident in some of the accusations, in which women do not dwell on their own stories in details but rely on the legitimacy acquired by other women in the movement (*ethos*), say they went through the same thing and use their platform to demand some change instead. Mia Kirshner is explicit about it:

> I could waste this precious space on HW by describing my own ordeal with him. An ordeal in a hotel room where he attempted to treat me like chattel that could be purchased with the promise of work in exchange for being his disposable orifice. But I'm not giving that man, a newly crowned figurehead of sexual abuse, the privilege of more ink. There are broader and more urgent issues to address. And if we don't address them now, I fear that when the headlines about Harvey Weinstein fade, what will remain is a disease in my own industry. (Kirshner, 2017)

Here, she does not give details, but rather positions her experience in relation to the other women's. She can only do that because other women did this legitimation work before her, so as to open the stage for other women to push a political agenda. This also shows in the nominalization process that can be found in some of the accusations:

> Little did I know it would become my turn to say no. No to opening the door to him at all hours of the night [...] No to me taking a shower with him. No to letting him watch me take a shower. No to letting him give me a massage. No to letting a naked friend of his give me a massage. No to letting him give me oral sex. No to my getting naked with another woman. No, no, no, no, no.... (Hayek, 2017)

> The details of what I have learned was not unique to me are now out there – the office tour that became an occasion to trap me in an empty meeting room, the begging for a massage, his hands on my shoulders as I attempted to beat a retreat... all the while not wanting to alienate the most powerful man in Hollywood. (Godbold, 2017)

Nominalization, evident in the -ing marker and in the use of the definite article *the*, happens when a "process [is] converted into a noun. It is reduced in the sense that some of the meaning one gets in a sentence is missing – tense, so there is no indication of the timing of the process; modality; and often an agent and/or patient" (Fairclough, 1989: 2004). In this case, the process has already been presented and exposed before by other women, it is something known—or considered to be—by the intended audience. With these nominalizations, what used to be the grammatical rheme of the utterances becomes the topic: it is no longer questioned and in need to be legitimized, but it is presented as a recognized fact. The rheme is the demands and claims they make for things to change.

Through these means, women therefore assert their authority as truth-tellers: they are reliable and can be trusted. Once their stories and the possibility that Harvey Weinstein might be a sexual predator was accepted, women were legitimate in denouncing the system and asking for change. They could then assert their authority to ask for change.

4.1.2   Asserting Their Authority as Truth-Leaders Asking for Change

This process is progressive: it is only when their authority as truth-tellers is attested that they can start asserting their authority as leaders. This is related to what Fairclough calls "relational modality": "Modality is to do with speaker or writer authority, and there are two dimensions to modality, depending on what direction authority is oriented in. Firstly, if it is a matter of the authority of one participant in relation to others, we have relational modality. Secondly, if it is a matter of the speaker or writer's authority with respect to the truth or probability of a representation of reality, we have expressive modality, i.e. the modality of the speaker/writer's evaluation of truth" (Fairclough, 1989: 126). Expressive modality can be conveyed through epistemic modals, but also when the speaker expresses an absolute commitment to the truth, notably through the use of simple tenses. The use of simple past tense and of the active voice that was mentioned above can therefore be considered to be features of expressive modality. Expressive modality is also found in WM's speeches: participants are adamant about the situation, as can be seen in the use of negations, simple tenses, and epistemic modals expressing a high probability of realization:

> In Washington DC, they don't want us to have dreams and to have a future. Republicans are saying 'We won't give you the DREAM act unless

you punish your parents, unless you give up being able to petition for your families.' And we say 'no'! We're one community, one nation, one family. (Angelica Salas, in WomensMarchLA2018, 2018b)

But in California, we're not just pushing back against attacks on voting rights, we're advancing voting rights, so we make it easy"; "in this country that we love, when we see injustice, we stand up, we take action, we march. When immigrants, or Muslims, or working men or women, or communities of colour, are targets of a tax, we stand up, we take action, we march. (Alex Padilla, in WomensMarchLA2018, 2018c)

Today we plant the seeds that will create a landscape that our children will not only survive in, but thrive in. (Eva Longoria, in WomensMarchLA2018, 2018e)

The use of those linguistic features leaves little place to challenge. They are stating things rather than opening a possible debate—which is in part due to the fact that their audience is on their side. Nevertheless, women asserting their authority as leaders have also to do with relational modality: the authority they feel they have to lead a movement for change in society and therefore the authority they feel they have to challenge the moral fabric of society. This is evident in the use of the root modal "should" and "must" in HW accusations and WM speeches. In doing so, they pass a moral judgement on the workings of society as it is. Once again, they are able to do so because their legitimacy in protesting was established with the HW case. It is important because, due to the HW case, they are in the limelight, and they have a platform that goes beyond feminist circles:

No woman should have to be subjected to this type unacceptable abuse. Women have the right to say no. (Mimi Haleyi, in Allred 2017c)

No woman should have to give up her dreams. No woman should be required to engage in sex in exchange for getting a job or keeping a job. (Allred, 2017b)

We should let their strength guide our way forward, which means beginning a larger conversation about the role economic inequality often plays in rape culture. (Marling, 2017)

Interestingly enough, the WM corpus includes only 8 occurrences of *should* compared to the 30 root uses of the modal in the HW sub-corpus. And yet, the log ratio for the semantic category "strong obligation or necessity" in Wmatrix for the WM sub-corpus shows that it is almost twice as high as it is in a reference corpus (log ratio of 0.86). The sense of strong obligation or necessity, which is significant in the sub-corpus, is therefore conveyed through other means, one of which is the root modal *must*:

This must be your cause too. (Eric Garcetti, in WomensMarchLA, 2018f)

Everyone who enjoys the privilege of voting in our elections must do so. (Eva Longoria, in WomensMarchLA2018, 2018e)

We must do more than march, we must act, we must act with strength, and purpose, and determination. […] We must ensure that our friends and family all over the country vote. We must vote regardless of party, we must vote of values, of truth, and compassion and justice. We must never forget that fighting, and win, is what we know how to do. (Lorry Jean, in WomensMarchLA2018, 2018h)

On the scale of root modality, *must* expresses a stronger sense of obligation than *should* does. Moreover, this is reinforced by external obligation linguistic markers, such as "need to" or "have to":

We have to reach out to our sisters who wear red baseball caps. […] We have to reach out to our sisters who are not in the streets today. (Alfre Woodard, in WomensMarchLA2018, 2018a)

We have to keep showing up […] we need everyone to work together. We must reach across cultural divide and recognise our power as an undivided force […] we need to take leadership […] we must amplify their voices as we learn from their experience […] we must remember our strength is in our unity. (Olivia Wilde, in WomensMarchLA2018, 2018j)

So we need to stand together! We need to stand proud. (Angelica Salas, in WomensMarchLA2018, 2018b)

It therefore appears that the shift from the HW case to the WM goes along with a shift from moral judgement and advice to a sense of obligation, both personal and impersonal. The movement is one that reaches out to the whole of society and extends the sense of responsibility.

This is reinforced by the use of pronouns, in particular the use of *you*. In the WM corpus, the personal pronoun *you* scores a LR of 1.87, which means that it is almost four times as frequent in the sub-corpus as it is in the reference corpus of American English. Speakers are calling out to the audience and to their responsibility:

What are we gonna do? You want 2018 to be better than 2017? We got to get everybody eligible, registered, and ready to roll. (Alfre Woodard, in WomensMarchLA2018, 2018a)

Speak with your vote, support the candidates who promise to build the city and the state and the country that you want to live in, that you want your daughters to live in. (Eva Longoria, in WomensMarchLA2018, 2018e)

We don't live in a theocracy! It's simply un-American! So, here's what we're gonna do. We're going to vote these traitors out! What are you going to do? (Ani Zonneveld, in Muslims For Progressive Values, 2018)

We need you to support us. (Dr Melina Abdullah, in WomensMarchLA2018, 2018d)

By resorting to the second-person pronoun *you* rather than the first-person pronoun *we*, the speakers display some form of authority over the audience, part of the relational modality described by Fairclough. The personal pronoun *we* creates more inclusiveness and in-groupness than the personal pronoun *you*, which is one of the means used by the movement to gather troops for the ideological struggle that is at stake here. Women therefore needed to establish their authority, first as truth-tellers and then as leaders, in order to engage in the struggle, the battlegrounds of which are ideological.

4.2   Ideological Struggle

4.2.1 Delegitimization of the Existing Ideology

The ideological struggle these women enter into starts with a delegitimization of the existing ideology, one in which women are held in an inferior position and in which their voices are not as valued as that of men. This delegitimization is evident in the overrepresentation of negation in the HW and the WM corpora. Indeed, the semantic category "negative"—which is essentially composed of the negation marker "not/n't"—scores 7th rank in the relative semantic tagging of both sub-corpora (with categories such as "pronouns" or "personal nouns" scoring higher). Negation is thus an important feature in the definition of this discourse, and the notion of counter-discourse seems appropriate: the discourse that women are building is built in direct and clear opposition to an existing situation and ideology. This means that the appraisal of the situation is negative, and speakers are calling for a change, both in the HW case and in the WM: "This has been the year we as women have said no more. We have said no more abuse, we have said no more fear, no more injustice and no more silence" (Nicole Richie, in WomensMarchLA2018, 2018i). This is confirmed by the choice of lexis they made, in particular in the HW accusations. The lexis that is used presents a certain framing that conveys a negative evaluation of the reality: women do not resort to euphemisms or to metaphors when telling their stories and do not tone down their language in order to spare the audience, as is usually the case when talking about taboo subjects (Allan & Burridge, 2006):

He then grabbed my hand and pulled me towards him and forced my hand onto his penis and held it there. (Heather Kerr, in Allred 2017b)

When I finished my pitch, I was obviously nervous, and he just kept asking to watch him masturbate. I told him I was leaving. He quickly got out of the tub, grabbed my forearm as I was trying to grab my purse, and he led me to his bathroom, pleading that I just watch him masturbate. (Louisette Geiss, in Allred 2017a)

Weinstein then proceeded to expose himself to Sivan and began to masturbate. Sivan said she was deeply shocked by Weinstein's behavior and was frozen and didn't know what to do or say. (Ali, 2017)

On the contrary, their accusations are very detailed and blunt. Their aim is not to spare the audience but to confront them about the situation and about the ideology of men such as HW. To do so, they rely on the established dichotomy between victim and aggressor, a dichotomy that is known to the audience and which leads them to feel for the women, who identify as the victims: "Victim", "predator" (Graham, 2017), "Unscathed" (Beckinsale, 2017), "I escaped 5 times" (Forlani, 2017), "invader", "felt trapped", "self-preservation", "a bug in a spider's web" (Erika Rosenbaum, in CBS Radio, 2017), "Coerced", "victim" (Anderson, 2017), "Predator", "prowl", "rampant predatory behaviour" (Nyong'o, 2017), "sly, sleazy smile" (Heather Kerr, in Allred, 2017b), "sociopaths", "torture" (Evans, 2017), "I had survived", "monster", "vice", "hurt" (Hayek, 2017), "literal trafficking or prostitution of young women" (Marling, 2017), "predator", "victim" (Godbold, 2017), and "serial predator" (Brock, 2017). They therefore frame their stories as situations of danger, sometimes life-threatening danger, in which they are the victims and in which HW is the predator. This participates in creating a negative evaluation of the situation and this is confirmed by the semantic tagging of the corpus: categories such as "violent, angry", "unsuitable", "no respect", or "unethical" have significant LR scores compared to the reference corpus—meaning that they are significantly more present in the corpus than in the reference corpus. Semantic tagging is important because it highlights the semantic trends of texts and points to the feeling discourse conveys on the whole to the audience. Here, the tagging identified participates in the delegitimization of the behaviour and ideology displayed by men such as HW. However, there are few occurrences of direct negative appraisal such as "this is bad"; on the contrary, this delegitimization is managed through positioning their stories in relation to an established social construct of what is good and what is bad. They therefore carry out a moral delegitimization of this pattern of behaviour and of the ideology that sustains it indirectly by confronting it to established social constructs. They appeal to the audience's empathy (*pathos*) to lead them to delegitimize the current ideology and in turn legitimate their own fight against it. They thus resort to what Jonathan Charteris-Black calls "conviction rhetoric", which is "grounded in ethical appeal and arouses emotions" (Charteris-Black, 2011: 10). Indeed, the emotions they are appealing to are grounded in morals and ethics: "Persuasion is about being right and only once the speaker has convinced the audience that he is right can the audience be said to have been persuaded. A prerequisite for being right is that the speaker gains trust by establishing his ethical integrity: when the people no longer trust their leader, any arguments or narratives that he offers will not be persuasive. The way that trust is established is by convincing the audience that the leader has the right intentions for the group and that he has their interests at heart" (Charteris-Black, 2011: 14). This is particularly obvious in one of the semantic categories identified by the software Wmatrix: "fear, bravery, shock", which is subdivided into two categories, one positive "bravery" and one negative "fear and shock". These two categories both score significantly in the LR, above 1.5, meaning that they are more than twice as frequent as in the reference corpus. This works to reinforce the empathy the audience feels towards those women who are presented as being brave in the face of the frightening situation they went through. By delegitimizing HW and the ideology he acted by and represents, they present themselves as morally worthy (*ethos*) of opposing and speaking out against it. They depersonalize their struggle: they do not only protest for their own sake, but the struggle they lead is ideological and moral, and as such, they enjoin their audience to side with them. The way they also depersonalize their struggle is through building a community from their shared experience.

4.2.2 Building a Community of Shared Experience and Political Action

This process is particularly evident in the use of pronouns that are made in the corpus: there is an evolution in the use of pronouns in the whole corpus, one that is characterized by a progressive shift from the personal pronoun "I" to the personal pronoun "we". This shift is operated through several stages.

In the HW corpus, the use of the first-person singular pronoun is significant. Indeed, the LR of "I" and of "me" in the sub-corpus is respectively 1.92 and 2.45, indicating that the occurrences of first-person singular pronouns are approximately 4 times as frequent in this sub-corpus as they are in the reference corpus. It is not only a case that personal pronouns are very frequent in any discourse, but something particularly striking in this case. This is relevant considering that these women speak out after having been silenced/silent for a long time: they take centre stage and make their voices and narratives heard. The movement therefore started with an emphasis on the personal. Nevertheless, already in the HW corpus, some sort of community of shared experience is being built. Indeed, in many accusations, a shift from "I" to "we" can be witnessed, by which women open up their individual experiences to the experiences of other women. They identify with other women and explicitly say so, thus creating a community of shared experience through empathy: they are not alone in this experience and many other women suffered the same abuse:

> It's part of what's holding so many of us back from sharing our stories. We don't want to be attacked for reading into something that may or may not have been there. We don't want to be looked at as weak for not being able to handle ourselves in a business run by men. We don't want to be defined as a 'Difficult Woman'. (Graham, 2017)

> "But why do so many of us, as female artists, have to go to war to tell our stories when we have so much to offer? I think it's because we, as women, have been devalued artistically to an indecent state"; "I hope that adding my voice to the chorus of those who are finally speaking out will shed

light on why it is so difficult, and why so many of us have waited so long". (Hayek, 2017)

Their voices and experiences become mingled with the voices and experiences of the other victims speaking out in this common "we", in a process of depersonalization that is essential in order to shift this moment—accusations against a lone individual, HW—into a movement, which is broader in scope and in claims. The individual stories are essential in legitimizing and grounding their claims for change, but it is necessary to link them to some social and political claims—and thus to externalize the accusations and claims—for the movement to be considered a social movement: "Under certain circumstances, members of certain disadvantaged groups do, in fact, engage in collective behavior in order to improve their situation. Social movements are a case in point. They have been defined, from a psychological point of view, as 'effort[s] by a large number of people to solve collectively a problem that they feel they have in common' (Toch, 1965, p.5)" (Simon et al., 1998: 646). This is very close to the consciousness-raising groups initiated by feminist groups, from which Carol Hanisch developed her theory about the personal being political. The conclusion of this theory is that if the different experiences of oppression that women suffer from in their daily lives are not personal phenomena but the results of structural, social inequalities, then it should not be up to individual women to try and solve these: the solution should be collective and the burden of change should rest on society. In the HW corpus, beyond the use of the personal pronoun "we", the lemma "woman/women" occurs 394 times, 304 of which in the plural form: if these discourses were only about the separate, individual experiences of abuse that the women telling their stories underwent, there would not be so many occurrences of the third-person reference "woman/women", and even less so in the plural form. There is therefore an attempt to link these personal experiences to one another and to the experiences of women in general.

This generalization/depersonalization shift that was initiated in the HW accusations was then expanded even further with the "me too" movement which opened up the movement, out of the Hollywood microcosm, to the whole of society (and even to many different societies across the world). With the expression "me too", women—and some men—victims of sexual abuse joined the community of shared experience; what is striking at this stage is that it is not the individual circumstances that matter anymore—the character limit imposed by Twitter does not allow victims to go into details—rather than the fact that this happened to yet another person, exemplifying the depersonalization shift that is operating between the HW case and the WM. Indeed, with the WM, the shift from the personal to the political seems complete as is evident in the use of the personal pronoun "we", which predominates in the sub-corpus. There are 282 occurrences of "I" against 478 occurrences of "we" in the WM corpus, by which we can clearly see the shift from the personal to the collective. It does nevertheless point to the importance of the individual voice: indeed, narratives of personal experiences of abuse still punctuate the different events of the movement, such as the Women's March or later in 2019 during the protest against Brett Kavanaugh's nomination to the Supreme Court of the United States. They never completely disappear, but they are not the main focus anymore as they were in the HW case; rather, they serve a larger purpose, that of grounding the claims they are making. However, past the HW case, the general takes precedence over the individual, as is explicit in the frequency of the personal pronoun "we" in the second sub-corpus. Not only are first-person plural pronouns more frequent than first-person singular pronouns, but they are significantly more used than in the reference corpus. In the WM corpus, the log ratio for the personal pronoun "we" is 2.98, meaning it is almost 8 times more frequent in the sub-corpus as it is in the reference corpus. What prevails is therefore the collective. Moreover, a shift in the reference of this pronoun operates at this stage. The "we" not only refers to a community of shared experience anymore, but rather to a broader community of responsibility: the community is political and refers to the people whose responsibility is to act in order to bring about change. It is to be remembered that the 2WM occurred a few months before the mid-term elections in the United States and there are many references to democracy and the democratic process of voting.

History will record in this most dangerous and baffling hour, how we stood, we organised, we reached across false boundaries and put our common purpose first. (Alfre Woodward, in WomensMarchLA2018, 2018a)

Seeing so many people do what we do as Americans. In this country that we love, when we see injustice, we stand up, we take action, we march. (Alex Padilla, in WomensMarchLA2018, 2018c)

We cannot be a great country until women not only have a seat at the table, but are actually seated at the head of the table. (Larry Wilmore, in WomensMarchLA2018, 2018g)

In these examples, it is clear that the reference of the personal pronoun "we" goes beyond the victims of sexual assault or even women in general. There is an equation of "we" with "the American people"; one of the chants of the March, and which was initiated by Alfre Woodard, is: "the people united will never be defeated" (Alfre Woodard, in WomensMarchLA2018, 2018a). The shift to the political is complete here: a dichotomy is created between the people assembled in the March, the Americans—and what is hinted at here is that they are the "true" Americans, defending democracy and their country's values ("It is so great to be out here again, a year after the first march, and seeing so many people do what we do as Americans. In this country that we love, when we see injustice, we stand up, we take action, we march" [Alex Padilla, in WomensMarchLA2018, 2018c])—and people such as Donald Trump ("Mr President" is also one of the most significantly frequent expressions of the sub-corpus) who are a threat to democracy. As a matter of fact, the word "country" is also significant in the corpus: the struggle is linked to the country's fate. As in Carol Hanisch's definition, the burden has shifted from women's shoulders to society. Speakers of the March are calling out to the audience and to their responsibility in making things change; this is also evident in the use of the personal pronoun "you" that is being made at the March, the LR of which is 1.87: it is almost 4 times as frequent as in the reference corpus. As was already mentioned above, leaders of the March are calling out to the responsibility of the audience in making sure that changes are made, through voting: "it's on you to fix this shit" (Dr Melina Abdullah, in WomensMarchLA2018, 2018d).

5   Conclusion

The struggle for authority and the ideological struggle that are at stake in the building of the counter-discourse and counter-ideology, if presented separately in this paper, are actually related and interdependent. One does not go without the other in this movement and it is the gradual and constant interplay of the two that turned the individual cases against HW into a fully-grown feminist movement. All those features and all those different texts form a network of texts that rely on one another. This was already alluded to in the HW accusations: women make references to the other accusations that are being made in this context. This is also the case with the WM discourses. Indeed, even if the WM opened up the debate around democracy and all the breaches against democracy, women's issues still hold centre stage, in a clear link with the HW case: the word "women" is the first most used lexical word in the WM corpus, and it is, after all, the *Women*'s March. Women's rights in the face of discrimination, the same that was defended in the HW case, become the standard for all other types of discrimination and abuse. In both corpora, speakers mingle elements of *logos*, *pathos*, and *ethos* in order to convince their audience of the legitimacy of their claims and to exhort them to take action. Emotions and reasons are constantly resorted to, once again in interrelation, which serves to legitimize the movement, to achieve consent with a large part of the population, not only people directly concerned by first denunciations, and thus to enter into ideological struggle

References

Ali, Y. (2017, October 9). TV Journalist Says Harvey Weinstein Masturbated in Front of Her. *The Huffington Post*. https://www.huffpost.com/entry/weinstein-sexual-harassment-allegation_n_59d7ea3de4b046f5ad984211.

Allan, K., & Burridge, K. (2006). *Forbidden words: Taboo and the censoring of language*. Cambridge: Cambridge University Press.

Allred, G. (2017a, October 10). *Gloria Allred Represents a New Accuser of Harvey Weinstein (Louisette Geiss)*. https://www.youtube.com/watch?v=O4x4vtuJKDs.

Allred, G. (2017b, October 20). *Gloria Allred brings forth a New Harvey Weinstein Accuser (Heather Kerr)*. https://www.youtube.com/watch?v=calxIty87vA&frags=pl%2Cwn.

Allred, G. (2017c, October 24). *Gloria Allred brings forward yet another Harvey Weinstein Victim*. https://www.youtube.com/watch?v=VFX-wWVOyjc.

Anderson, A. (2017, October 16). *Instagram*. https://www.instagram.com/p/BaUBLfFFMDb/?utm_source=ig_embed.

Beckinsale, K. (2017, October 12). [Instagram]. https://www.instagram.com/p/BaJiAhyn7Y5/.

Bloor, M., & Bloor, T. (2007). *The practice of critical discourse analysis: An introduction*. London: Hodder Arnold.

Bohner, G. (2002). Writing about rape: Use of the passive voice and other distancing text features as an expression of perceived responsibility of the victim. *British Journal of Social Psychology, 40*(4), 515–529.

Boltanski, L., Darré, Y., & Schiltz, M.-A. (1984). La Dénonciation. *Actes de La Recherche En Sciences Sociales, 51*(1), 3–40.

Brock, Z. (2017, October 7). Harvey Weinstein and I at the Hotel du Cap. *Medium*. https://medium.com/bullies-assholes-i-have-known/harvey-weinstein-and-i-at-the-hotel-du-cap-57e5883cde36.

CBS Radio. (2017, October 13). 'He really took something from me': Montreal actress Erika Rosenbaum says Harvey Weinstein assaulted her. *The Current*. https://www.cbc.ca/radio/thecurrent/the-current-for-october-13-2017-1.4352029/he-really-took-something-from-me-montreal-actress-erika-rosenbaum-says-harvey-weinstein-assaulted-her-1.4353082.

Charteris-Black, J. (2011). *Politicians and rhetoric*. London: Palgrave Macmillan press.

Epstein, D., & Goodman, L. A. (2018). Discounting credibility: Doubting the testimony and dismissing the experiences of domestic violence survivors and other women. *University of Pennsylvania Law Review, 167*(2), 399–461.

Evans, A. (2017, October 14). Did rejecting Harvey Weinstein's sinister advances shut down my career—And my husband's? *The Telegraph*. https://www.telegraph.co.uk/women/life/did-rejecting-harvey-weinsteins-sinister-advances-shut-career/.

Fairclough, N. (1989). *Language and power*. London: Longman.

Fairclough, N. (2010). *Critical discourse analysis: The critical study of language* (2nd ed.). Abington: Routledge.

Forlani, C. (2017, October 12). [Twitter]. https://twitter.com/claireaforlani/status/918518181894930432.

Godbold, L. (2017, October 9). My encounter with Harvey Weinstein and what it tells us about Trauma. *Aces Connection*. https://www.acesconnection.com/blog/my-encounter-with-harvey-weinstein-and-what-it-tells-us-about-trauma.

Graham, H. (2017, October 10). Heather Graham: Harvey Weinstein implied i had to have sex with him for movie role (EXCLUSIVE). *Variety*. http://variety.com/2017/film/columns/heather-graham-harvey-weinstein-sex-for-movie-role-1202586113/.

Hanisch, C. (1969). The personal is political. In S. Firestone & A. Koedt (Eds.), *Notes from the second year: Women's liberation* (pp. 76–78). New York. Available at: https://library.duke.edu/digitalcollections/wlmpc_wlmms01039/.

Hayek, S. (2017, December 13). Opinion | Harvey Weinstein Is My Monster Too. *The New York Times*. https://www.nytimes.com/interactive/2017/12/13/opinion/contributors/salma-hayek-harvey-weinstein.html.

Kantor, J., & Twohey, M. (2017, October 5). Harvey Weinstein paid off sexual harassment accusers for decades. *The New York Times*. https://www.nytimes.com/2017/10/05/us/harvey-weinstein-harassment-allegations.html.

Kirshner, M. (2017, October 13). I was not protected from Harvey Weinstein. It's time for institutional change. *The Globe and Mail*. https://www.theglobeandmail.com/opinion/i-was-a-victim-of-harvey-weinstein-but-we-have-to-focus-on-the-future/article36584019/.

Marling, B. (2017, October 23). *Harvey Weinstein and the Economics of Consent*. The Atlantic. https://www.theatlantic.com/entertainment/archive/2017/10/harvey-weinstein-and-the-economics-of-consent/543618/.

McIntyre, D., & Walker, B. (2019). *Corpus stylistics: Theory and practice*. Edinburgh: Edinburgh University Press.

Muslims For Progressive Values. (2018, January 25). *Ani Zonneveld*. https://www.youtube.com/watch?v=GBHlE5KKgFA.

Nyong'o, L. (2017, October 19). *Lupita Nyong'o: Speaking Out About Harvey Weinstein.* https://www.nytimes.com/2017/10/19/opinion/lupita-nyongo-harvey-weinstein.html.

Rapp, C. (2010). Aristotle's rhetoric. In E. N. Zalta (Ed.), *The Stanford encyclopaedia of philosophy* (Spring 2010). Metaphysics Research Lab, Stanford University. https://plato.stanford.edu/archives/spr2010/entries/aristotle-rhetoric/.

Rayson, P. (2002). *Matrix : A statistical method and software tool for linguistic analysis through corpus comparison.* Lancaster: Lancaster University. http://ucrel.lancs.ac.uk/people/paul/publications/phd2003.pdf.

Simon, B., Loewy, M., Stürmer, S., Weber, U., Freytag, P., Habig, C., … Spahlinger, P. (1998). Collective identification and social movement participation. *Journal of Personality and Social Psychology, 74*(3), 646–658.

Simpson, P., Mayer, A., & Statham, S. (2010). *Language and power* (2nd ed.). Abington: Routledge.

WomensMarchLA2018. (2018a, January 25). *Alfre Woodard.* https://www.youtube.com/watch?v=Ye82gnfPhTE.

WomensMarchLA2018. (2018b, January 25). *Angelica Salas Executive Director CHIRLA.* https://www.youtube.com/watch?v=x3snBjSwXEw.

WomensMarchLA2018. (2018c, January 25). *CA Secretary of State Alex Padilla.* https://www.youtube.com/watch?v=dDRnN-VQQkE.

WomensMarchLA2018. (2018d, January 25). *Dr Melina Abdullah introduced by Sophia Bush.* https://www.youtube.com/watch?v=pxuL64xW9fY.

WomensMarchLA2018. (2018e, January 25). *Eva Longoria.* https://www.youtube.com/watch?v=36QlEN8aDi8.

WomensMarchLA2018. (2018f, January 25). *LA Mayor Eric Garcetti introduced by Viola Davis.* https://www.youtube.com/watch?v=UVdinBcfsCs.

WomensMarchLA2018. (2018g, January 25). *Larry Wilmore—Women's March Los Angeles 2018.* https://www.youtube.com/watch?v=XynuLD7lI3U.

WomensMarchLA2018. (2018h, January 25). *Lorri Jean—Women's March Los Angeles 2018.* https://www.youtube.com/watch?v=Asxyi4_Yddo.

WomensMarchLA2018. (2018i, January 25). *Nicole Richie—Women's March Los Angeles 2018.* https://www.youtube.com/watch?v=hmWWa65U_Zs.

WomensMarchLA2018. (2018j, January 25). *Olivia Wilde.* https://www.youtube.com/watch?v=coaOQp5Ah8s.

The Discursive Representation of Violence in the Context of the Migration Crisis in Europe: A CDA Case Study on the Discursive Support of Non-violence in the Media Reporting on the Chemnitz Events

Natalia Borza

1 Introduction

On the night of the city festival, a German-Cuban carpenter was stabbed to death by three immigrants in Chemnitz, Saxony, in 2018. The murder led to immediate silent marches and protests in Chemnitz, and soon numerous German people assembled from other cities too to express their disapproval of Merkel's open-door policy. The protests triggered counter-demonstrations and the police was deployed to keep the two groups apart. As German citizens took to the streets over several days to voice their opinions, the German foreign minister, Heiko Maas, who feared that pictures of riots would damage Germany's reputation[1] urged

---

[1] *The Guardian*, 28 August 2018.

N. Borza (✉)
Department of Humanities and Social Sciences, Pázmány Péter Catholic University, Budapest, Hungary

87

P. Anesa and A. Fragonara (eds.), *Discourse Processes between Reason and Emotion*, Postdisciplinary Studies in Discourse, https://doi.org/10.1007/978-3-030-70091-1_5

citizens to join a free rock concert organized as a celebration of non-violence in Chemnitz. Tension on the streets of Chemnitz captured international attention, and the English-language online media reported on the events. The present research investigates how a lexical field (Fowler, 1991) was created around the theme of violence promoting the culture of non-violence in high-quality English-language online news articles. The investigation aims to shed light on the discursive means—appealing both to reason and to emotions—that made the mobilization of people by the German foreign minister appear reasonable. Accordingly, answers are sought to the following research questions.

RQ1:   To what extent is the semantic field of violence discursively represented in the English-language online media accounts reporting on the Chemnitz events?

RQ2:   What characterizes the discursive representation of violence regarding social *actors* and social *actions* in the newspaper articles under investigation?

To answer these questions, the study will first outline the events that took place in Chemnitz at the end of summer 2018 (2.1) against the backdrop of the Free State of Saxony, which is often referred to as the stronghold of extremism (2.2). Since the mobilization for the free rock concert was legitimized through a discourse emphasizing non-violence as a key virtue, the notion of non-violence is sketched within the frame of civil disobedience and pacifism, where it historically developed (2.3). Finally, the nature of violence with a positive connotation is considered (2.4). The method section explicates the methods of quantitative (3.1) and qualitative (3.2) data analyses used in the research. The results of the research are discussed along the following lines: the extent of the presence of the semantic field of violence (4.1—RQ1), the rate at which social actors are described as violent (4.2—RQ2), the discursive representation of social actors (4.3—RQ2) and that of social actions (4.4—RQ2). The paper ends with summative concluding remarks.

2   Background

2.1   The Chemnitz Events

In the Free State of Saxony in East Germany, a murder committed by immigrants led to hundreds of mourners congregating in the city centre of Chemnitz, and demonstrations ultimately attracted thousands of protesters over several days. The large number of protesters were finally outnumbered in the city by tens of thousands enjoying a free concert. To understand how the number of people on the streets rose exponentially after the immigrants' fatal stabbing, I will first give a summary timeline of the most crucial events in Chemnitz. To present this outline, I draw on the chronological report in the locally present, regional German-language state media, MDR[2] Sachsen, which is a member of the nationwide state media broadcaster, the ARD.[3] The MDR Sachsen report on the Chemnitz covers a period of one year, recounting the events from 26 August 2018 until 22 August 2019. The present summary focuses on the main events of the first nine days, until the last reports on the rock concert celebrating non-violence came out in the English-language online media. Information that is not directly relevant to the escalation of the events was not included in this overview, while pieces of information which help comprehending the events in their context but were published outside the boundary of the nine-day time period of the research were provided in the footnotes.

In the early hours of the morning (26 August, Sunday), several people of various nationalities were involved in a fight in the inner city of Chemnitz. Three people, aged between 33 and 38, were taken to hospital with serious injuries. One of them, a 35-year-old man, died in the hospital. An Iraqi man (22) and a Syrian man (23)[4] were arrested for allegedly

---

[2]MDR is the abbreviation of Mitteldeutscher Rundfunk.

[3]ARD stands for Arbeitsgemeinschaft der öffentlich-rechtlichen Rundfunkanstalten der Bundesrepublik Deutschland.

[4]During the trials held in 2019, the Syrian defendant, Alaa S., was found guilty of manslaughter and grievous bodily harm. Consequently, he was sentenced to nine and a half years in prison. As the defence lawyer has lodged an appeal at the Federal Court of Justice, at the time of publication of this research the verdict is not yet legally binding.

having stabbed the 35-year-old man with a knife several times.[5] The city council and the organizers of the city festival decided to bring the festival to a premature end as a mark of piety and condolence with the relatives of the victim. In the afternoon, approximately 800 hundred people gathered spontaneously around the Karl Marx monument, close to the spot where the murder was committed. The assembly was not registered, however, and gradually dispersed before the evening fell.

Next day (27 August, Monday) the murder victim was identified as Daniel H.,[6] a carpenter. The arrest warrant for the alleged perpetrator was illegally leaked. For the evening, two demonstrations were registered in the city centre, one by the right-leaning Citizens' Movement Pro Chemnitz,[7] and a counter-demonstration by the alliance "Chemnitz Nazifrei". Around 5,000 people took part in the protest march, while an estimated 1,000 people participated in the counter-demonstration. About eight in the evening, the two groups of protesters became violent, and bottles and fireworks were thrown. However, before eleven in the evening, the situation calmed. Four participants of the protest march were injured by 15–20 attackers from the counter-demonstration. The police made a thorough video recording of the demonstrations.

On Tuesday (28 August) the police opened ten cases against people who made the Hitler salute in public during the demonstrations, which is a constitutional offence and thus illegal action in Germany. By Wednesday (29 August) the prosecution announced that one of the suspects had already been convicted on several counts. On Saturday (1 September) around 8,000 people took part in the demonstrations in Chemnitz, and an additional 3,000 people protested against them at a

---

[5]The third perpetrator, Farhad Ramazan Ahmad, apparently an Iraqi man (22), whose asylum application was rejected in January 2017 and thus should have been deported from Germany, escaped. Although an international arrest warrant was issued against Farhad R., he had not been found by the time the trials were held in 2019. The allegedly Iraqi man was not unknown to the police, as he had been convicted for several crimes he committed in Germany, such as bodily harm, drug trafficking, theft, trespassing, property damage, insult, threat, resistance to law enforcement officers, and even stabbing (*Source* Freie Presse, 13 September 2018; Welt, 5 September 2018).

[6]The German press guards the anonymity of people involved by revealing the first letter of the family name only. The English-language press, however, published the full name of the victim, Daniel Hillig.

[7]Pro Chemnitz became a municipal political party in Saxony in 2019.

counter-demonstration under the banner of "Herz statt Hetze" or "Heart not Provocation". There were 18 injuries, and the protests remained mostly peaceful according to the police. Sunday (2 September) saw around 1,200 protesters, and again the demonstrations were peaceful. Monday's (3 September) #wirsindmehr (there are more of us) free concert, which was organized against violence, racism, and xenophobia, attracted around 65,000 visitors. The event remained peaceful.

2.2   Extremism and Violence in Saxony

In order to see why so many concert goers considered Chemnitz as a dangerous hotspot, it is worth examining how Chemnitz is viewed regarding extremism and violence. When reporting on the events in Chemnitz, the English-language newspaper accounts not only locate Chemnitz on the map of Germany, but also introduce the Free State of Saxony as well. The reason for this could be that people in Saxony are described to have distinct Saxon self-confidence, which seems to lead them on their own way (Jesse, 2016). Even during the period of the German Democratic Republic (GDR), it was in Saxony where a noticeable movement for democracy developed against the socialist regime, and the Free State was considered to be the centre of the "Peaceful Revolution" (Pickel, 2016). Although people in Saxony (91%) appreciate democracy[8] (Pickel, 2016), for decades Saxony has been regarded as the stronghold of extremism (Backes, 2016). Extremism in Saxony can be found at both ends of the spectrum: the far-right is typically associated with the movement PEGIDA (Patriotic Europeans against the Islamization of the West) and Dresden, while the far-left is linked with active radical left-wingers in Leipzig. Vorländer et al. warn that although Saxony is described as manifesting "strong right-wing extremist structures", the presence of "xenophobic, nationalistic and neo-National Socialistic orientation" is not higher in the population of Saxony than in the other former GDR states and they also add that Dresden has an average "concentration of xenophobic orientation" compared to other

---

[8]In the German context, the term "extremist" refers to someone who has a negative attitude to democracy per definitionem (Pickel & Decker, 2016).

large cities, even Western German ones (2018: 171–173). Bearing these statistics in mind, it is understandable that most of the PEGIDA demonstrators viewed their protest as "a form of democratic self-empowerment of the citizens against the rule of a media-political elite detached from the people" (Vorländer et al., 2018: 184) rather than a form of extremist activity.

Examining the politically motivated crimes committed in Saxony between 2013 and 2019, the far-right committed more crimes (between 1,672 and 2,468 each year) than the far-left (between 671 and 1,385 each year) (Staatsministerium des Innern, Freistaat Sachsen, 2019). The same tendency can be seen all over Germany: politically motivated crimes were 1.56–1.93 times more frequently committed by the far-right than by the far-left (Bundesministerium des Innern, für Bau und Heimat, 2020). With regard to the types of crimes, however, it was the far-left which committed bodily harm and murder 1.16–2.18 times more often than the far-right. Historically, the typical target of the far-left is the police, representatives of the state, bankers, businessmen and all those who epitomize society (Mannewitz et al., 2018: 119). On the other hand, the type of crime which considerably increased the criminal statistics of the far-right in Germany was hate crime, where anti-Semitic crimes played a minor role (Mannewitz et al., 2018: 130). At the same time, compared to other states of the former GDR, the number of crimes committed by the far-right in Saxony is not outstandingly high (Backes, 2016), it ranks even behind Saxony-Anhalt and Mecklenburg-Vorpommern (Vorländer et al., 2018: 173).

As the Chemnitz events were sparked by a murder and severe bodily harm committed by immigrants, it is also worth examining the rate of crimes committed by immigrants in Saxony. In the last decade, the number of immigrants entering Germany has soared dramatically. In 2013 nearly 17,000 immigrants entered Saxony, a figure which almost quadrupled in 2016 (Staatsministerium des Innern, Freistaat Sachsen, 2017). In 2018, when the Chemnitz events took place, almost 60,000 immigrants crossed the border of the Free State. The massive number of immigrants arriving and staying each year meant that by 2017, 4.6% of those living in Saxony were immigrants (Statistisches Landesamt des Freistaates Sachsen, 2017). In the last four years, between 2016 and

2019, immigrants committed close to 20,000 crimes annually,[9] statistics which do not even include the violation of immigration law (Staatsministerium des Innern, Freistaat Sachsen, 2019). Besides the high rate of crime, the types of crimes immigrants committed were also varied, including crime against life,[10] bodily harm,[11] theft,[12] robbery,[13] sexual assault[14] and drug offences.[15]

2.3   Non-violence

Let us now turn our attention to the notion of non-violence, which was one of the buzz words in the invitation to the rock concert. Non-violence is the means of practising civil disobedience and pacifism. As the name implies, the idea of non-violence entails refusing to resort to violence, that is, it rejects the "behaviour involving physical force intended to hurt, damage, or kill someone or something" (Oxford Dictionary, 2020). Both in its everyday use and in legal terminology, the notion of violence covers actions involving physical force (Cambridge Dictionary, 2020; Longman Dictionary, 2020; Macmillan Dictionary, 2020; Merriam-Webster, 2020; Oxford Dictionary, 2020). Applying non-violence serves civil disobedience, the conscientious public violation of law or government policy in order to bring about social or political change (Bigalke, 2011). In the middle of the nineteenth century, the first modern advocate of the duty of civil disobedience, Henry David Thoreau (2004) drew an analogy between the problems of government and the friction of a machine, thus urging principled people to become counter friction that might stop the ill-working of the government. Civil disobedience can be employed to support pacifism, "the belief that humanity can live peaceably" (Marsden,

---

[9]2016: 18,828; 2017: 19,769; 2018: 18,695; 2019: 16,439.

[10]2016: 16; 2017: 31; 2018: 19; 2019: 29.

[11]2016: 3,098; 2017: 3,285; 2018: 3,003; 2019: 2,749.

[12]2016: 6,561; 2017: 6,112; 2018: 5,669; 2019: 4,486.

[13]2016: 282; 2017: 284; 2018: 305; 2019: 347.

[14]2016: 232; 2017: 290; 2018: 349; 2019: 280.

[15]2016: 1,142; 2017: 1,513; 2018: 1,815; 2019: 1,701.

2011) by way of settling disputes and conflicting interest through nego-
tiations. Pacifists, who seek to "avoid inflicting any kind of physical or
psychological harm on the oppressor" (Orosco, 2018), reject warfare and
object to military service as a natural consequence of their opposition to
violence.

Considering the pattern of civil disobedience in general and pacifism
in particular, the Chemnitz case follows a completely different trajectory. In civil disobedience movements and in the practice of pacifism,
it is the civilian who protests against the law or government policy by
way of a non-violent non-cooperation with the state, in order to call
policy-makers' attention to a social or political issue. In the Chemnitz
events, however, it was not the counter-demonstrating civilians who
came together to raise their voices, but the foreign minister, Heiko Maas,
who mobilized citizens to protest in the name of non-violence. Additionally, the urged counter-protest of the counter-demonstrators in Chemnitz
was not targeted at a government policy, as is typically the case in non-
violent protests, but it was aimed against fellow German citizens voicing
their opinion in protest marches.

2.4   Prosocial Violence

Finally, let us consider the range within which violence is accepted.
On a consensual basis, social psychology conceptualizes aggression—
behaviour directed towards another person that is carried out with
the proximate intent to cause physical or psychological harm (Krahé,
2013)—as a negative form of social behaviour. Aggressive behaviour is
placed in stark contrast with forms of prosocial behaviour, ones that
benefit another person (Eisenberg et al., 2015). Forming a dichotomous
relation between the notions of aggression and prosocial behaviour makes
the concept "prosocial violence" genuinely invalid for social psycholo-
gists. Yet Gross warns that although our culture supports non-aggression,
there are situations when prosocial aggression is required, and in which
even "cultural processes teach and sustain it" (2017: 191). Disciplining
children and wrong-doers, acting assertively and practising self-defence
are listed among such situations. The underlying common feature behind

exhibiting aggressive behaviour in these situations is the application of instrumental aggression with "socially constructive and desirable consequences", as the American Psychological Association (2020) defines it. To raise awareness of the possibility of violence with a positive connotation from the point of view of the community, Rogish and Grossman (2013) employed the metaphor of the "sheepdog" for prosocially minded people who use violence without pathology but with empathy, and with "a sincere drive toward a greater good" (Coghlan, 2010: 103). Police officers are prime examples of sheepdogs as they need to be comfortable with aggression and violence when acting in the interests of society at large, that is, for the security of the sheep, in Rogish and Grossman's terminology.

3   Method

In order to gain insights into how violence connected to the events in Chemnitz was represented in the English-language online media, the present research follows the Critical Discourse Analytical (CDA) approach, which considers language as social practice (Fairclough & Wodak, 1997). As such, CDA does not focus on texts as "objects of inquiry" (Wodak & Meyer, 2001: 2) in isolation, but investigates both the social process and the social structures in which the text was produced. CDA focuses particularly on the relation between language and power with the aim of "demystifying discourses by deciphering ideologies" (Wodak & Meyer, 2001: 10). The critical element of the approach denotes making visible the "interconnectedness of things" (Fairclough, 1985: 747). Among the major characteristics of CDA, van Dijk underlines the importance of disclosing what is implicit or hidden "in relations of discursively enacted dominance", which in discourse analytical practice means the uncovering of the "strategies of manipulation, legitimation, the manufacture of consent and other discursive ways of influencing the minds [...] of the people in the interest of the powerful" (1995: 18). In van Leeuwen's phrasing, CDA can provide "an incontrovertible account of the way representations of social reality select, interpret, and evaluate social reality" (2018: 2). The present analysis accords with the view demonstrated by Chouliaraki and Fairclough (1999) questioning the neutrality of media institutions, which purport to reflect states of affairs disinterestedly.

The study applies the mixed-methods approach, which involves collecting, analysing and interpreting both quantitative and qualitative data in order to provide a more comprehensive understanding of the research problem (Baran & Jones, 2019; Bergman, 2008; Cresswell, 2014; Leech & Onwuegbuzie, 2009) through a methodological pluralism (Johnson & Onwuegbuzie, 2004) when investigating the same underlying phenomenon.

3.1   Quantitative Data Analysis

To discover the extent of the presence of the semantic field of violence (RQ1), Wmatrix, a corpus annotation software developed by Lancaster University, was applied (Rayson, 2008). The automated tool uses the USAS category system for tagging and grouping words and multi-word expressions together which are related to the same mental concept. The USAS semantic tagset, which is based on Tom McArthur's Longman Lexicon of Contemporary English (McArthur, 1981), is hierarchically organized into twenty-one major discourse fields, further subdivided into 232 category labels. Data about the semantic domain of violence can be found directly in three of the major discourse fields ("General and abstract terms", "Emotional actions, states and processes" and "Government and the public domain") and in three category labels ("Damaging and destroying" tagged as A1.1.2, "Calm/Violent/Angry" tagged as E3 and "Crime, law and order" tagged as G2.1). While one more category label ("Respect" tagged as S7.2) potentially provides information about the semantic field of violence, inasmuch as its absence is connected to the act of intimidation or the use of physical force. To show the overuse of items in a particular corpus compared to a standard reference corpus, Wmatrix applies log-likelihood statistics as well as log ratio. Log-likelihood (LL) values computed by the annotation software are statistically significant over 7, as the cut-off for 99% confidence of significance is 6.63 (Rayson, 2008). By contrast, log ratios are the binary log of the ratio of relative frequencies, which reveal how big the difference is between two corpora considering the item under investigation (Hardie, 2014). A one-point increase in the Log Ratio value represents a doubling in the size of the difference between the two corpora for the item under scrutiny. The present analysis examined both LL values, in order to see the strength of the evidence for the difference of the two corpora, and log ratios, with the aim of discovering the difference in size in the use of the items between the two corpora. As a reference corpus, the British National Corpus (BNC) Sampler Written (SW), a general, synchronic, monolingual corpus was selected, which includes almost one hundred million orthographic words.

The corpus under investigation embraces English-language online newspaper articles from quality press which reported on the invitation of the German foreign minister, Heiko Maas, to a free rock concert organized as a celebration of non-violence in Chemnitz in 2018. Sensationalist journalism, articles of the tabloid press were not examined. The concert and the motives underlying its organization were reported on in the English-language quality press for three days (2 September–4 September 2018) in five articles from four quality media outlets: *The BBC*, *The Guardian*, *The Telegraph* and *The Times*. The five articles built a corpus of 2890 words in total. Table 1 gives detailed information about date of publication and length.

Table 1 The corpus under investigation

Date of publication	Newspaper	Chemnitz Concert Corpus Code	Length of the article
2 September, 2018 Sunday	*The Telegraph*	CCC 1	600 words
2 September, 2018 Sunday	*The Guardian*	CCC-2	568 words
3 September, 2018 Monday	*The Guardian*	CCC-3	609 words
3 September, 2018 Monday	*The Times*	CCC-4	786 words
4 September, 2018 Tuesday	*The BBC*	CCC-5	327 words

3.2   Qualitative Data Analysis

To examine the discursive manner in which social actors and social actions are represented, van Leeuwen's (2008) sociosemiotic inventory was applied. Sociosemiotics, the branch of linguistics which focuses on semiotic systems in social practice (Hodge & Kress, 1988), postulates that language is generated by the social context in which it occurs (Danesi, 2000). Accordingly, it studies how semiotic systems are shaped by social interests and ideologies. Additionally, it investigates the power of the human processes of signification and interpretation (semiosis). This is markedly relevant for van Leeuwen's taxonomy, which not only categorizes discursive representations, but also describes the cognitive and emotional effect a particular representation creates for the reader. One of the major divisions within this taxonomy is between inclusion and exclusion. Inclusion refers to the discursive representation wherein a social actor is explicitly named in relation to an action, while in the case of exclusion the social actor is merely implicitly present in the text. The less radical form of exclusion, backgrounding, does not mention the social actor in connection with an act, since a clear inference can obviously be made from other part(s) of the text. Conversely, the radical form of exclusion, suppression, makes no reference anywhere in the text to the social actor in question in association with the action. In contrast to inclusion, which emphasizes the actor and his or her responsibility for the action, exclusion deemphasizes the actor and lessens or hides his or her responsibility for the particular action. Radical exclusion, otherwise known as suppression, removes a voice from the discourse. Furthermore, suppression has the power to take away an avenue of dispute and may even block access to knowledge.

Social actions, on the other hand, can either be represented dynamically, which is grammatically realized in a verbal form, or represented statically as if they were qualities or entities rather than processes. The first type of representation is termed activation, the latter is called deactivation in van Leeuwen's (2008) taxonomy. Activation places the social action in the foreground of the text, while deactivation backgrounds it. Deactivation can also serve the purpose of legitimation and delegitimation or the classification and labelling of social actions.

In order to find the characteristics of the discursive representation of violence regarding social actors and social actions (RQ2), words and expressions which convey the meaning of violence, that is the behaviour involving physical force intended to hurt, damage or kill someone or something (Cambridge Dictionary, 2020; Longman Dictionary, 2020; Macmillan Dictionary, 2020; Merriam-Webster, 2020; Oxford Dictionary, 2020), were tagged. It is important to note that the core of the meaning of violence, as defined by all the five authoritative dictionaries, is the use of physical force. Given that the essential feature of violence is physical action, notions which lack this active, coercive element cannot be classified as violent. As a result, sentiments, dispositions, attitudes, qualities of the character and mental states were not tagged as violent unless physical force was also included. Lexical units that are conventionally associated with potential violence yet do not contain physical force were not tagged as violent in the analysis. In this manner, the feeling or thought of disapproving or being afraid of people from other countries (*xenophobia*) and the belief that different racial or ethnic groups can be distinguished by distinct characteristics, qualities and abilities (*racism*) were not tagged as violent. Similarly, as the intense feeling of dislike (*hate, outrage, horrified*) involves no physical action, it was not tagged as violent either. The lexical unit "hate" can denote a hostile action as a modifier (e.g. *hate attack*), however, no such use appeared in the corpus.

4   Results and Discussion

4.1   The Extent of the Presence of the Semantic Field of Violence

The automatic semantic analysis of the corpus showed that the online newspaper articles made abundant use of the conceptual field of violence (RQ1). All the category labels relevant to the lexical field of violence show a statistically significant difference (LL > 7) compared to the British National Corpus (BNC) Sampler Written (SW).

Table 2 displays the LL values for each category label day by day, where it can be seen that the lowest LL value (LL = 9.72) is clearly above

Table 2 LL and log ratio values of the category labels relevant to 'violence'

Category label	Publication date	Newspaper	Code	Log Likeli-hood (LL)	Log ratio
Crime	2 September, 2018 Sunday	The Telegraph The Guardian	CCC-1 CCC-2	9.72	2.61
Calm/Violent/Angry	2 September, 2018 Sunday	The Telegraph The Guardian	CCC-1 CCC-2	63.21	3.29
	3 September, 2018 Monday	The Guardian The Times	CCC-3 CCC-4	49.38	3.16
Damaging/destroying	2 September, 2018 Sunday	The Telegraph The Guardian	CCC-1 CCC-2	25.19	3.10
	4 September, 2018 Tuesday	The BBC	CCC-5	10.09	3.77
No respect	3 September, 2018 Monday	The Guardian The Times	CCC-3 CCC-4	11.49	5.60

the significance threshold, while the highest LL value (LL = 63.21) is massively above this threshold. This shows that there is firm evidence for the difference between the two corpora regarding the lexical field of violence. The size of the difference between the two corpora regarding the semantic domain of violence is revealed by the Log Ratio values. The Log Ratio value of the category label "Crime" (2.61) indicates that the newspapers under investigation apply lexical items in this lexical domain four times more frequently than the reference corpus does. To an even greater extent, the semantic field "Calm/Violent/Angry" (Log Ratio 3.29; 3.16) occurs eight times more densely in the newspaper articles than in the BNC SW. In a similar manner, the semantic field of "Damaging and destroying" (Log Ratio 3.10; 3.77) appears eight times more frequently in the newspaper articles than in the corpus of general English. Even more drastically, the conceptual field of "No respect" (Log Ratio 5.60) emerges thirty-two times more frequently in the newspaper articles than in the reference corpus.

4.2   Social Actors Narrated as Violent

Let us now observe the characteristic features of the discursive representation of social actors and actions (RQ2) within the semantic field of violence. The examined online newspaper articles apply 93 lexical items in the conceptual field of violence, which delineate five groups of social actors: the far-right, immigrants, the far-left, "we", and the police. Table 3 shows the raw number of occurrences and the ratio as a percentage of the lexical items. It is worth noting that the ordinary demonstrator is not among the social actors of the narrative. The reason for this might be argued to lie in the fact that regular demonstrators tend not to be violent, thus their social actions were outside the focus of the research investigating the discursive representation of violence. However, the lack of the presence of the ordinary protestors among the social actors is in fact due to the discursive tendency to blend the group of ordinary protestors and the far-right into one single group in the narrative, see Sect. 4.4.

Nearly two-thirds of the lexical items in the semantic field of violence (60%) appear in association with the group of people denoted as far-right or neo-Nazis. Lexical items in the semantic domain of violence are used approximately three times less often (18%) in relation to immigrants. Lexical items in the field of violence are linked with the group denoted as far-left five times less often (12%) than with the group denoted as far-right. The articles construct the social actor "we", to which fewer than one tenth of the lexical items (8%) are connected in the conceptual field of violence. The smallest number of lexical items in the lexical domain of violence is associated with the police (2%).

Considering how frequently violence is associated with the above five social actors in the discourse of the online newspaper articles, it is the group labelled by the media as far-right which is described as the

Table 3 Lexical items in the semantic field of violence regarding the social actors

Social actor	Raw number (and percentage) of lexical items
Far-right/Neo-Nazis	56 (60%)
Immigrant	17 (18%)
Far-left	11 (12%)
'We'	7 (8%)
Police	2 (2%)
ALL	93 (100%)

most violent. Violence is far less frequently emphasized with other social actors, such as immigrants and the far-left. The discrepancy is created by the narrative, which marginally reports on the violent acts committed by immigrants, the murder itself and the act of stabbing three other people. Violence committed by immigrants is not in the focus of the narration of any of the articles. In the same way, the online articles which mention violence committed by the far-left—such as throwing bottles and fireworks at demonstrators and the police, or causing injuries in several cases—do not repeat this piece of information. In contrast, violence committed by the far-right tends to be reiterated several times in all the news accounts leading to a disproportionality in the rate of violence committed by the social actors in the narration.

4.3   The Discursive Representation of Social Actors: Inclusion and Exclusion

After discovering the lopsidedness of the rate at which the various social actors are described as violent in the media, let us examine the ways how the various social actors are represented within the lexical field of violence regarding the patterns of inclusion and exclusion in the articles.

The group of people labelled by the press as far-right is as frequently included (41%) as backgrounded (43%) in the articles (see Table 4). The reason for the high rate of backgrounding may lie in the fact that the

Table 4 Inclusion and exclusion of the social actors in the semantic field of violence

Social actor	Inclusion (%)	Exclusion: backgrounding (%)	Exclusion: suppression (%)
Far-right/Neo-Nazis ($n = 56$)	41	43	16
Immigrant ($n = 17$)	65	6	29
Far-left ($n = 11$)	100	–	–
'We' ($n = 7$)	100	–	–
Police ($n = 2$)	100	–	–

group is frequently mentioned in the articles and the mere use of inclusive referencing would create an unnecessarily repetitive, abundant and overcommunicative style for the reader. One sixth of the references to the same group of people is suppressed (16%). The continual suppression of social actors develops a narrative in which the agents of violence are not clearly specified. It is not stated explicitly but merely to be assumed that the "37 possible offences" [CCC-2], the "bodily harm" [CCC-2] and the "resistance against law enforcement officers" [CCC-2] were committed by the group of people labelled as far-right. The articles do not provide information about the extent to which other social actors (the far-left, immigrants or "we") were involved in these violent actions. The lack of precise attribution implies that all the violence was committed by the far-right.[16]

On the other hand, immigrants are typically referenced inclusively (65%), and only one fifteenth of their referencing is backgrounded (6%). The need for the low rate of backgrounding can be explained by the scarcity of information imparted about this group of social actors by the media. Besides reporting on the "alleged" or "suspected" crimes they committed [CCC-1, CCC-3, CCC-4, CCC-5] and their "alleged" countries of origin (Syria and Iraq) [CCC-2, CCC-4], the articles convey no more information about the immigrants. Moreover, since this piece of information does not appear repeatedly in the articles, the narrative is comprehensible without using backgrounding. Referencing of immigrants is suppressed in nearly one-third of the cases (29%), which results in a narrative that de-emphasizes that the "stabbing" [CCC-1, CCC-2, CCC-3, CCC-5] and the "death" [CCC-1] was committed by immigrants. Veiling the social actors of these fatally violent actions hides the responsibility of the perpetrators in the narrative.

The referencing of the other three groups of social actors, the far-left, "we" and the police, is entirely inclusive, there are no examples of backgrounding or suppression. In the case of the group labelled as far-left no backgrounding or suppression is needed, as the media narration in

---

[16]The implication does not have a valid basis. The German-language press reported (27 August) that 15–20 counter-protestors caused bodily harm to four far-right demonstrators.

this regard is extremely brief, giving succinct information without repetition. Providing clearly stated inclusive referencing, the accounting of this group of social actors is strictly limited to the time and space of the events that took place in the inner city of Chemnitz. This stands in contrast with the narrative about the social actors labelled as far-right, where violent incidents that happened at other times, in other parts of the city or even in other cities were tentatively connected to the group of social actors present at the demonstrations, thus increasing the rate of violence of the far-right in the narrative.

As regards the referencing of the group of social actors labelled as "we", neither backgrounding nor suppression is required as facts about this group of social actors are underreported. Besides emphasizing the quality of preference for tolerance, the social actor "we" is more defined through its expressed enemy, namely the far-right, than through its own distinctive identity. This is why the hashtag of the social actor, "wirsindmehr" (there is more of us), specifies the group with a quantity, while their exact quality remains opaque in the narration.

Finally, the referencing of the police relies on mere inclusion, as the narrative gives little mention of them, stating that they "deployed water cannon and armoured vehicles" [CCC-4]. The scarceness of information about the police, which results from the narratives' lack of focusing on this group of social actors, makes it entirely unnecessary to use backgrounding or suppression.

4.4   The Discursive Representation of Social Actions

Having seen the ways in which the various social actors are represented discursively within the lexical field of violence regarding the patterns of inclusion and exclusion, let us examine the discursive representations of the social actions within the same semantic field with regard to activation and deactivation.

In the articles under investigation, the representation of the social actions of the group labelled as far-right is fairly balanced in terms of activation (41%) and deactivation (56%), see Table 5.

Table 5 Activation and deactivation of the social actions in the semantic field of violence

Social actor	Activation	Deactivation: objectivation	Deactivation: descriptivization
Far-right/Neo-Nazis (n = 56)	23 (41%)	29 (52%)	4 (7%)
Immigrant (n = 17)	3 (18%)	14 (82%)	–
Far-left (n = 11)	3 (27%)	8 (73%)	–
'We' (n = 7)	4 (57%)	3 (43%)	–
Police (n = 2)	2 (100%)	–	–

The use of activation versus deactivation (objectivation and descriptivization) can have a modifying effect on the narrative in various ways. Activation has the property of foregrounding the social actor and thus intensifying the responsibility of this social actor for a given action. In the newspaper accounts, several instances of activation increase the role of the social actors labelled as far-right in criminal activities. For example, the activation of the alleged[17] pursuit, "mobs have chased foreigners" [CCC-2], magnifies the answerability of the far-right. Also, the narration activates the action considered to be criminal under German law, "people are displaying the Hitler salute" [CCC-1, CCC-4], through which it strengthens the role of the same group of social actors for the offence. Similarly, the activation of yelling, "shouts foreigners out" [CCC-4], which is a punishable slogan in the Free State of Saxony,[18] adds to the

---

[17]As the police made thorough video recordings of the protests, Michael Kretschmer, Minister President of Saxony, firmly stated that "There was no mobbing, no Pogrom or chasings" of foreigners in Chemnitz. Heinz Eggber, former Interior Minister of Saxony, reinforced the same opinion. Hans-Georg Maaßen, President of the Federal Office for Constitutional Protection [Verfassungsschutzpräsident], Germany's domestic security agency's chief, expressed his doubts about the authenticity of the video showing the pursuit, which was published on the Facebook site of AntifaZeckenbiss. Maaßen also added that it was "targeted misinformation with the possible aim of distracting publicity from the murder in Chemnitz" (*Source* MDR Sachsen). "Publicly contradicting" (BBC, 24 September 2018) to what Chancellor Angela Merkel and her government's spokesman, Steffen Seibert had previously declared about the chasings of foreigners in Chemnitz led to a political fallout, and in consequence Maaßen was dismissed from the Federal Office for Constitutional Protection in less than two weeks' time (*Source* MDR-Sachsen).

[18]The slogan "Ausländer raus" is forbidden and punishable in the Free State of Saxony according to §130 StGB (Strafgesetzbuch), the criminal code in Germany (Landesamt für Verfassungsschutz Sachsen, 2016).

accountability of the far-right. Besides intensifying responsibility, other instances of activation in the accounts, e.g. "German journalist [...] had been threatened by protesters" [CCC-1], also have the potential to blend the far-right and ordinary people demonstrating against murder on the streets and against Merkel's open-border policy into one single, homogeneous group, the protesters. As an effect on the reader, the implied number of people involved in violence increases in the narrative, and so does the sense of the rate of violence during the events. An additional result of the blending is that ordinary people exercising their right of freedom of assembly and their right of free speech are characterized as neo-Nazis in the accounts. In the discourse around the call for the rock concert, the activation goes beyond the space and time of the events that happened in the inner city of Chemnitz, which vaguely generalizes the threat of far-right violence without any spatial or temporary limits: "for all of those people who have been attacked by neo-Nazis" [CCC-2]. Again, the generalization expands the magnitude of the violence associated with the far-right in the narrative. Several instances of the activations with regard to the actions of this social actor use agent deletion by passivation e.g. "Hitler salute was displayed" [CCC-1, CCC-4], "an Afghan man was attacked" [CCC-1], "one of the MDR crews was attacked" [CCC-], "18 people were injured" [CCC-2]. Due to the agent deletion, the reader is not provided with clearly stated information as to who carried out these actions. The narrative implies that the agency is to be attributed to the far-right, but the extent to which this social agent was accountable is left ill-defined.

In connection with the social agent labelled as far-right, the narrative uses a considerable amount of deactivation (59%), mostly in instances of objectivation (52%), and occasionally descriptivizations (7%). The objectivations have the effect of making the narrative blurred from several points of views. It remains indistinct what the social actors did exactly when "riots" [CCC-1, CCC-4] or "violence" [CCC-1, CCC-2, CCC-3, CCC-4] are mentioned in the articles. The notion of violence appears to be used in the narrative as an evaluative term with a negative connotation. The lack of active verb forms in the accounts concerning the "hunting for foreigners" [CCC-1] also leaves it unclear when such actions took place. Similarly, the question of who exactly committed

"37 possible offences" [CCC-2], "bodily harm" [CCC-2], "property damage" [CCC-2] and "resistance against law enforcement officers" [CCC-2] is left unspecified. Objectivations such as "fears of clashes" [CCC-1], "growing concerns that skirmishes could break out in other cities" [CCC-4] leave room for reporting on actions which never took place, but were mere speculation. Similarly, the discursive representation of people marching as "prone to violence" [CCC-3] predicts destructive social actions in the future. The forecast of speculative objectivations strengthens the sense of violence linked to the far-right in the narrative. Furthermore, the objectivation of the martial metaphor "Chemnitz [...] has become a battleground" [CCC-4] makes the threat of violence even more intense and belligerent in the account of these events.

The instances of descriptivization regarding the social actions of the far-right in the semantic field of violence have the same effects as the objectivations. The adjective "turbulent" [CCC-4], in describing the protests, is a very imprecise way to describe these social occurrences, but it does add to the connotation that the social agent created an increasingly violent confusion. The participle clause "armed with flares and German flags" [CCC-4] is a descriptivization that reinforces the image of war through a metaphor in the discursive representation of the events. Although flags are not used for fighting, the choice of the word "armed" metaphorically insinuates a militant behaviour on part of the far-right.

The discursive representation of the social actions connected to the next social actor, immigrants, is mostly deactivations (82%), with only few instances of activations (18%) in the narrative. The activated forms in connection with the immigrants are verbs which denote undergoing suffering, such as "an Afghan man [...] also escaped serious injury" [CCC-1] or "sustained light injuries" [CCC-2]. As activations have the capacity to increase the responsibility of the social actor, it is the hardship and the victimhood of the immigrants which are emphasized in the narration. The one single activation regarding immigrants which does not fall into the lexical field of distress and victimhood comes in a report on another case which did not occur in Chemnitz. Within the scope of the events that took place in Chemnitz, all the social actions in the semantic domain of violence related to immigrants are deactivations, or more specifically, objectivations. The various forms of objectivations such as "fatal stabbing" [CCC-1, CCC-2, CCC-3, CCC-5], "death" [CCC-1, CCC-4], "suspected stabbing" [CCC-1] and "killing" [CCC-1, CCC-4, CCC-5] offer the discursive possibility of omitting the social actor. As a consequence, two of the articles fail to mention in their caption and brief summary of the events that the "killing" [CCC-1] and "death" [CCC-4] were caused by immigrants. Besides making it possible to omit any explicit reference to the social actor, the use of objectivation lessens the responsibility of the social actor in the narrative. Thus, the extensive use of objectivation in the narration has the effect of diminishing the liability of the immigrants for their criminal deeds.

The social actions of the group labelled as far-left are discursively represented with a similarly low rate of activations (27%) and massive deactivations (73%) as the social actor immigrants. The activations of the narrative show the actions of this group of people to be violent e.g. "have clashed" [CCC-4] and vicious i.e. "were […] arming themselves with stones" [CCC-1]. The latter activation uses a military metaphor, which in contrast to the military metaphor applied to the far-right, is not merely symbolic. The stones of the far-left are physical objects that were gathered with the intention of using them as weapons in order to hurt others, while the flags of the far-right are symbols of unity, that of belonging to a nation and a shared community. Yet, the narrative of the articles does not create a sense of imminent danger caused by the far-left, as the reporting on their violence remains metaphorical rather than providing a concrete account of the physical assaults committed. Ironically, the free rock concert programme, which was organized in the name of non-violence, also involved violence connected to the far-left. Using activation, the news accounts reported that the lyrics of one of the performing bands, the punk band Feine Sahne Fischfilet, has the potential to "incite violence against the police" [CCC-4]. Despite the manifest presence of aggression in the lyrics against law enforcement officers, the narrative of the online newspapers does not discredit the free rock concert, nor does it label the concert violent. The various deactivations such as "fears of clashes", "violence" give a vague account of the social actions of the far-left by failing to describe precisely the violent deed they committed. Furthermore, the deactivations in reference to the explicit call for aggression of the lyrics of the performing punk band e.g. "street violence" [CCC-3], "hurling stones at the police" [CCC-3], "advocating far-left violence" [CCC-5] do not call into question the non-violent nature of the free rock concert.

The discursive representation of the social actions of the group "we" displays a balanced ratio of activation (57%) and deactivation (43%) in the semantic field of violence. As it is the negative qualities of the Other and the positive characteristics of Us that tend to be emphasized in the narrative (van Dijk, 1998), it is somewhat surprising that the in-group should be connected with social actions of violence. The reason for linking Us with the semantic field of violence, which is considered to be an unfavourable characteristic, is that the narratives illustrate Us as inherently non-violent through the use of negation in the activation: we belong to a generation which "didn't have to fight" for freedom, the rule of law and democracy [CCC-1, CCC-3]. On the other hand, the narrative urges Us to resort to violence when it comes to our sense of comfort, which needs to be thoroughly overcome: "we will have to vanquish it" [CCC-4]. That is, the narrative paradoxically applies the discourse of violence in its activations when insisting that people take sides against violence. The deactivation of the narrative, however, explicitly demands of Us that we should be violent, by citing the foreign minister, Heiko Maas, who "calls for citizens to become more active in the fight" [CCC-2]. The violent confrontation, which is otherwise clearly an unacceptable norm in the context of the narrative, is discursively legitimized by the belief in egalitarianism. Namely, the use of violence is regarded as an acceptable means as long as it is directed against the notion according to which people belonging to different ancestral or ethnic groups can be distinguished based on their distinct characteristics, that is, against "racism" [CCC-2]. This incendiary discourse is cautious enough to demand active violence from the public against a way of thinking rather than against a certain group of people, thus it does not fall into the category of hate speech.

It is only through activations (100%) that the social actions of the police are discursively represented. Some of the activations mentions the social actor explicitly, "police deployed water cannon and armoured vehicles" [CCC-4], while another instance uses agent deletion by passivation, "water cannons and riot police were deployed" [CCC-1]. The deletion does not have the effect of hiding the social agent, as it is obvious from the context that it was the police who applied water cannons. The narrative of the newspaper articles does not disapprove of the use of violence by the police. At the same time, it does not directly approve of the use of violence either, by discursively evaluating it as prosocial due to its maintenance of public order. This implies that prosocial violence carried out by the police is among the accepted norms and values of the narrative, and is taken for granted.

5   Conclusion

The present research investigated how a lexical field (Fowler, 1991) was created around the theme of violence promoting the culture of non-violence in high-quality English-language online news articles regarding the events in Chemnitz (2018). The conceptual field of violence was applied 4–32 times more often in the articles than in the reference corpus, BNC SW (RQ1). The representation of social actors was disproportionate in the narrative (RQ2). Most of the lexical items expressing violence were associated with the far-right (60%), while violence was linked to immigrants three times less often, and to the far-left five times less often. The reason for this disproportionality was the focus of the articles: the actions of the far-right were reiterated in all the articles, while the deeds of the far-left were not, and the fatally violent actions of the immigrants were reported on only marginally.

The discursive examination of the social actors and their actions within the semantic field of violence (RQ2) allows us to make the following observations about how the narrative represents the different social actors.

1. Regarding the far-right, the narrative

    – implies that they committed all the violent actions in the city of Chemnitz and in Germany (suppression);
    – increases their responsibility for violence (activation);

- blends them with ordinary German protesters into one homogeneous group, which A) increases the sense of the threat of violence in Germany, and B) depreciatively labels ordinary people as neo-Nazis (activation);
- extends time and space, which increases the sense of their threat (activation);
- conveys information without clarity, implying that they committed all the violence in Chemnitz (agent deletion by passivation);
- uses the term "violent" in an evaluative manner (with an obviously negative connotation) rather than imparting precise information (objectivation);
- reports on possible, speculative future events, which increases the perceived level of violence in Germany (objectivation)
- implies their uncontrolled violence (descriptivization).

2. Regarding immigrants, the narrative

- deemphasizes and even omits mentioning their responsibility for the fatal stabbing (backgrounding and deactivation);
- reports on their sufferings and victimhood (activation).

3. Regarding the far-left, the narrative

- sublimates their concrete violent actions into a metaphor, making their violence appear unreal and thus not dangerous (activation);
- implies that their violence is not harmful: it is merely art or entertainment (activation and deactivation);
- conveys information imprecisely, implying that it was the far-right who committed all the violence in Chemnitz (deactivation).

4. Regarding "us", the narrative

- assures that we are genuinely non-violent (activation);
- paradoxically uses military language in order to take sides against violence (activation);
- calls for violence, which is legitimized by targeting it against racism (deactivation).

5. Regarding the police, the narrative

– takes prosocial violence (the maintenance of order) for granted (activation).

The overuse of the conceptual field of violence, the quantitatively disproportionate representation of the social actors and the effects of the implications of the different representation of the social actions and social actors all add up to support for the German foreign minister's encouragement, mobilizing "us" to attend the free rock concert.

References

Backes, U. (2016). Politisch motivierte Gewalt in Sachsen. In G. Picke & O. Decker (Eds.), *Extremismus in Sachsen* (pp. 27–37). Leipzig: Edition Leipzig.

Bergman, M. M. (2008). *Advances in mixed methods research: Theories and applications.* London: Sage.

Baran, M. L., & Jones, J. E. (2019). *Applied social science approaches to mixed methods research.* Hershey, PA: IGI Global.

Bigalke, R. J., Jr. (2011). Civil disobedience. In G. T. Kurian (Ed.), *The encyclopedia of political science.* Washington, DC: CQ Press.

Chouliaraki, L., & Fairclough, N. (1999). *Discourse in late modernity: Rethinking Critical Discourse analysis.* Edinburgh: Edinburgh University Press.

Coghlan, T. E. (2010). *Role interference and moral distress in the subjective experience of deep undercover law enforcement operatives.* Boca Raton, FL: Dissertation.com.

Cresswell, J. W. (2014). *Research design: Qualitative, quantitative, and mixed method approaches.* London: Sage.

Danesi, M. (2000). *Encyclopedic dictionary of semiotics, media, and communication.* Toronto: University of Toronto Press.

Eisenberg, N., Spinrad, T., & Knafo, A. (2015). Prosocial development. In: M. E. Lamb & R. M. Lerner (Eds.), *Handbook of child psychology and developmental science* (Vol. 3: Social, Emotional and Personality Development). New York: Wiley.

Fairclough, N. (1985). Critical and descriptive goals in discourse analysis. *Journal of Pragmatics, 9,* 739–763.

Fairclough, N., & Wodak, R. (1997). Critical discourse analysis. In T. van Dijk (Ed.), *Discourse studies: A multidisciplinary introduction* (pp. 258–284). London: Sage.

Fowler, R. (1991). *Language in the news.* London: Routledge.

Friese, H., Nolden, M., & Schreiter, M. (2019). *Rassismus im Alltag. Theoretische und empirische Perspektiven nach Chemnitz.* Bielefeld: Transcript.

Gross, R. (2017). *Psychology in historical context: Theories and debates.* Abingdon: Routledge.

Hardie, A. (2014). Log Ratio—An informal introduction. ESRC Centre for Corpus Approaches to Social Science. http://cass.lancs.ac.uk/log-ratio-an-inf ormal-introduction/.

Hodge, R., & Kress, G. (1988). *Social semiotics.* Cambridge: Polity.

Jesse, E. (2016). Regionale politische Kultur in Sachsen. In N. Werz & M. Koschkar (Eds.), *Regionale politische Kultur in Deutschland. Fallbeispiele und vergleichende Aspekte* (pp. 189–210). Wiesbaden: Springer.

Johnson, R. B., & Onwuegbuzie, A. J. (2004). Mixed methods research: A research paradigm whose time has come. *Educational Researcher, 33,* 14–26.

Landeskriminalamt Sachsen. (2016). *Augen auf! Sehen – Erkennen – Handeln. Rechtsextremistische Symbole, Kennzeichen und Organisationen.* Dresden: Landesamt für Verfassungsschutz Sachsen.

Krahé, B. (2013). *The social psychology of aggression.* Hove, UK: Psychology Press.

Leech, N. L., & Onwuegbuzie, A. J. (2009). A typology of mixed methods research designs. *Quality & Quantity, 43,* 265–275.

Mannewitz, T., Ruch, H., Thieme, T., & Winkelmann, T. (2018). *Was ist politischer Extremismus? Grundlagen, Erscheinungsformen, Interventionsansätze.* Frankfurt/M.: Wochen Schau Verlag.

Marsden, L. (2011). Pacifism and conscientious objection. In G. T. Kurian (Ed.), *The encyclopedia of political science* (pp. 1165–1166). Washington, DC: CQ Press.

McArthur, T. (1981). *Longman lexicon of contemporary English.* London: Longman.

Orosco, J. A. (2018). Pacifism as pathology. In A. Fiala (Ed.), *The Routledge handbook of pacifism and nonviolence* (pp. 199–210). New York: Routledge.

Pickel, G. (2016). Eine sächsiche politische Kultur des Extremismus? Politishce Einstellungen in Sachsen im Bundesländervergleich und ihre politikwissenschaftliche Einordnung. In G. Picke & O. Decker (Eds.), *Extremismus in Sachsen* (pp. 16–26). Leipzig: Edition Leipzig.

Pickel, G., & Decker, O. (2016). *Exremismus in Sachsen. Eine Kritische Bestandsaufnahme*. Leipzig: Edition Leipzig.

Rayson, P. (2008). From key words to key semantic domains. *International Journal of Corpus Linguistics, 13*(4), 519–549. https://doi.org/10.1075/ijcl.13.4.06ray.

Rogish, S., & Grossman, D. (2013). *Sheepdogs: Meet our nations warriors*. West Bend: Delta Defense LLC.

Thoreau, H. D. (2004). *Walden, life in the woods, and on the duty of civil disobedience*. Princeto: Princeton University Press.

van Dijk, T. A. (1995). Aims of critical discourse analysis. *Japanese Discourse, 1*, 17–27.

van Dijk, T. A. (1998). *Ideology*. London: Sage.

van Leeuwen, T. (2008). *Discourse and practice: New tools for critical discourse analysis*. Oxford: Oxford University Press.

van Leeuwen, T. (2018). Moral evaluation in critical discourse analysis. *Critical Discourse Studies*. https://doi.org/10.1080/17405904.2018.1427120.

Vorländer, H., Herold, M., & Schäller, S. (2018). *PEGIDA and new right-wing populism in Germany*. Cham, Switzerland: Palgrave Macmillan.

Wodak, R., & Meyer, M. (2001). *Methods of critical discourse analysis*. London: Sage.

Statistics

Bundesministerium des Innern, für Bau und Heimat (2020). *Politisch motivierte Kriminalität im Jahr 2019. Bundesweite Fallzahlen*. https://www.bmi.bund.de/SharedDocs/downloads/DE/veroeffentlichungen/2020/pmk-2019.pdf?__blob=publicationFile&v=8.

Staatsministerium des Innern, Freistaat Sachsen (2017). *Kriminalitätsentwicklung im Freistaat Sachsen im Jahr 2017*. https://www.polizei.sachsen.de/de/55703.htm.

Staatsministerium des Innern, Freistaat Sachsen. (2019). *Kriminalitätsentwicklung im Freistaat Sachsen im Jahr 2019*. https://www.polizei.sachsen.de/de/71564.htm.

Statistisches Landesamt des Freistaates Sachsen. (2017). *Statistiken*. https://sab.landtag.sachsen.de/de/service/statistiken/statistiken-6757.cshtml.

Websites

APA: Dictionary of the American Psychological Association. (2020). https://dictionary.apa.org/prosocial-aggression.

BBC. (2018, September 24). Angela Merkel apologises over Maassen's controversial promotion. https://www.bbc.com/news/world-europe-45626815.

Cambridge Dictionary. (2020). https://dictionary.cambridge.org/dictionary/english/violence.

Freie Presse. (2018, September 13). Der dritte Mann: Wer ist der flüchtige Verdächtige der Bluttat von Chemnitz? https://www.freiepresse.de/der-dritte-mann-wer-ist-der-fl-chtige-verd-chtige-der-bluttat-von-chemnitz-artikel10310345.

Longman Dictionary. (2020). https://www.ldoceonline.com/dictionary/violence.

Macmillan Dictionary. (2020). https://www.macmillandictionary.com/dictionary/british/violence.

MDR Sachsen. (2019, August 20). Der Todesfall Daniel H. - eine Chronologie der Ereignisse in Chemnitz. https://www.mdr.de/sachsen/chemnitz/chemnitz-stollberg/chemnitz-ausschreitungen-chronologie-demonstrationen-100.html.

Merriam-Webster. (2020). https://www.lexico.com/definition/violence.

Oxford Dictionary. (2020). https://www.lexico.com/definition/violence.

The Guardian. (2018, August 28). German police criticised as country reels from far-right violence. https://www.theguardian.com/world/2018/aug/28/german-police-criticised-as-country-reels-from-far-right-violence.

Welt. (2018, September 5). Er gab sich reuig – jetzt wird er überall gesucht. https://www.welt.de/politik/deutschland/plus181432774/Chemnitz-Asylantrag-des-dritten-Verdaechtigen-war-abgelehnt-worden.html.

Gender-Based Violence in Italian Local Newspapers: How Argument Structure Constructions Can Diminish a Perpetrator's Responsibility

Erica Pinelli and Chiara Zanchi

1   Introduction

In Italy, gender-based violence (henceforth GBV) is a pervasive phenomenon. As the 2015 ISTAT report shows, 149 Italian women were killed intentionally in 2014, with 109 killings qualifying as femicides (*femminicidi*, in Italian) and perpetrated within the nuclear family, by the victims' current or previous intimate partner or by a family member

This research was carried out within the crowdfunded project *WordsMatter* (https://sites.google.com/unipv.it/wordsmatter/). The article is the result of close collaboration between the two authors. For academic purposes only, Erica Pinelli is responsible for Sects. 3 and 4, and Chiara Zanchi for Sects. 1, 2, 5, and 6.

E. Pinelli (✉) · C. Zanchi
University of Pavia, Pavia, Italy
e-mail: erica.pinelli@unipv.it

© The Author(s), under exclusive license to Springer Nature Switzerland AG 2021
P. Anesa and A. Fragonara (eds.), *Discourse Processes between Reason and Emotion*, Postdisciplinary Studies in Discourse,
https://doi.org/10.1007/978-3-030-70091-1_6

of hers.[1] The number of victims grows exponentially if one considers GBV in all of its forms: in 2014, almost 6.8 million women between 16 and 70 years of age experienced GBV. From the 2015 ISTAT report, a picture of the Italian situation emerges in which it is clear that GBV is still widespread among people of all social statuses. However, the report points out that in 2009-2014 there were signs indicating that the incidence of GBV was decreasing while women's—particularly young women's—awareness of it was growing.

More recent data offers a discouraging glimpse of how GBV is still perceived by young Italians. The ANSA report of November 2018 notes that '56.8% of boys and, lamentably, 38.8% of girls, believe that *the female* is at least *partly responsible* for the violence she has suffered' (translation and emphasis are ours).[2] This evidence suggests that younger generations still embrace dominant cultural values that partly relieve the perpetrators of their responsibility. The 2019 ISTAT report on GBV, however, is more comforting concerning the extent to which gender-based stereotypes and perceived motivations of violence can cross demographic and social boundaries.[3] Even though 54.6% of Italians interviewed in 2018 agreed with at least one among the GBV stereotypes taken into consideration (i.e. 'If women do not want to have sexual intercourse, they always have means to avoid it'; 'Women can invite sexual violence by the way they dress'; 'If a woman experiences sexual violence when she is drunk or high, she shares responsibility for

---

[1]ISTAT is the *Italian National Institute for Statistics* (https://www.istat.it); the 2015 report on violence against women can be read and downloaded at this address: https://www.istat.it/it/files//2015/06/Violenze_contro_le_donne.pdf. In Italy, as well as in the other European Union member states, the legal category of femicide/feminicide does not exist (sometimes, the terms femicide and feminicide are distinguished in the literature, cf. e.g. Karadole, 2012; other authors opt for other expressions, see e.g. 'intimate partner violence/femicide' in Monckton-Smith, 2012, 'intimate murder' in Wykes, 1995, and 'patriarchal terrorism' in Johnson, 1995). In the *International Classification of Crime for Statistical Purposes* 1.0 (https://unstats.un.org/unsd/statcom/doc15/BG-ICCS-UNODC.pdf), drawn by the UNODOC in 2015, femicide is characterized as "[…] the intentional killing of a woman for misogynous or gender-based reasons" (p. 32).

[2]The *Agenzia Nazionale Stampa Associata* (ANSA, literally 'Associated Press National Agency') is the leading wire service in Italy. The cited report can be found here: http://www.ansa.it/canale_saluteebenessere/notizie/stili_di_vita/2018/11/30/violenza-donne-per-4-giovani-su-10-dipende-anche-da-lei_b834f656-fdf2-4a0c-8de5-2d6c6dfcfc82.html.

[3]The 2019 ISTAT report can be viewed here: https://www.istat.it/it/archivio/235994.

the act'; 'Accusations of sexual assault are often false'.), this percentage decreased with decreasing age, with higher levels of education, and among females. In addition, the 2019 ISTAT report points out that most Italians (77.7%) indicated that 'regarding women as possessions' is the most relevant motivation for GBV. This percentage also increased among young women (18–29 years old) and women with higher amounts of education.

In spite of these positive signals, slowly fading gender-based stereotypes are still depressingly alive in Italian society. Such stereotypes are mirrored in sexual power asymmetries between men and women. An evaluation of these asymmetries is related in the *Gender Gap* report, which ranks countries according to the gap calculated between how women and men are treated in four key social areas, specifically, health, education, economy, and politics, to compare the extent of gender equality across the world.[4] In 2018, Italy ranked at 70th position: in the European region only Greece, Malta, and Cyprus ranked lower.

Thus, given that GBV is pervasive in Italy, that gender-based stereotypes are still deeply rooted in the Italian society, and that such stereotypes are still reflected in asymmetrical power relationships between men and women, we are now in the position to hypothesize that women are also likely to be subject to linguistic misrepresentation in public discourse in general, and in media discourse in particular. As Scott (1990) noted, such misrepresentation is an ever-present feature of asymmetrical power relationships and personalized violence. Coates and Wade (2007: 512) added that 'as a general rule, the more strident the abuse of power, the more effectively it must be justified or concealed by perpetrators and their supporters'. Meyers (1997: 22) pointed out that media represent a 'framework that supports the dominant ideology while marginalizing, trivializing and constructing as deviant or dangerous any challenge to it'. Although an isolated instance of unfair discourse has no power per se, the repetition of subtly biased narrative patterns (or 'discursive frameworks') gives the media a pervasive and powerful influence on its audience's conceptualizations of events (e.g. Fairclough, 1989;

---

[4]The 2018 *Gender Gap* report can be seen here: http://www3.weforum.org/docs/WEF_GGGR_2018.pdf.

Meyers, 1997). Using Schaeffer's (1990: 2) terminology, the thematization and routinization of GBV results in a *sensus communis*, that is, a body of expectations about how a certain event operates in the public sphere (see also Fagoaga, 1994). It is worth emphasizing that we do not necessarily contend that any media or journalists deliberately conspire against weaker social groups, and specifically women in this case. Misrepresentation may well result from different factors, including institutionalized professional imperatives (e.g. operating within a very busy writing schedule and strict word limits), commercial interests (e.g. having to write articles catering to a particular audience), or unconscious gender-based stereotypes. All these phenomena may contribute to making the journalists opt for well-worn, routinized, and frequently unjust formulas to report GBV and other kinds of violent events.

Dating from the works of Lakoff (1973, 1975) onward, particularly regarding sexually based power asymmetries, it has been argued that language and discourse both contribute to constructing sexual inequality and mirror its presence in the society (Graddoll and Swan, 1989: 164). Goddard and Saunders (2000) even spoke of sexist language as a form of 'textual abuse'. This linguistic abuse, be it overt or covert, actualizes GBV by habituating the use of discursive frameworks that create or enhance gender-based stereotypes and the consequent personal and institutional power asymmetry between men and women. Such discursive frameworks result in what Mills (2008) defined as 'indirect sexism' (cf. also Benwell's 2007 'new sexism', Lazar's 2005 'subtle sexism', Williamson's 2003 'retro-sexism'): namely, an array of indirect linguistic strategies, such as humour, presuppositions, metaphors, collocations, and others, which build narratives that imply an unbalanced power relationship between men and women.

Overt textual abuses are typically perpetrated in the media by lexical choices. Consider the following two examples from our corpus (described at length in Sect. 3):

(1) *Coltellate per soffocare un **amore*** (GS, Mar 2017) 'Knives to smother **love**'
(2) *Il giovane, **vittima** della sua **gelosia*** (GS, May 2018) 'The young man, **victim** of his **jealousy**'

In (1), the journalist wrote that *coltellate* 'knives' have the agency to smother an *amore* 'love': these lexical choices, *coltellate* 'knives' and *amore* 'love', conceal the true perpetrator and victim of this voluntary killing. The victim is a real woman, not an abstract emotion. In parallel, the perpetrator is a man, not an inanimate instrument. In addition, *amore* 'love' highlights that the perpetrator killed his partner in the thrall of this emotion. The latter abusive discursive frame emerges more clearly in (2), where the perpetrator is even deemed the *vittima* 'victim' of an emotion, specifically, of his *gelosia* 'jealousy'. Previous studies on how GBV and femicide are represented in the written media have focused on lexical words or collocations, which overtly construct abusive discourses reaffirming sexual inequality: see, e.g. Erlich (2003) and O'Hara (2012) on English; Santaemilia and Maruenda (2014) on Spanish.

Regarding Italian news reports, Abis and Orrù (2016) carried out a qualitative analysis of 143 articles dating back to the period from 2010 to 2015 and narrating femicides: they particularly focused on (i) descriptions relating to victims, their status in the relationship, and their physical traits; (ii) the circumstances, such as professional and mental health issues, that triggered the crime; (iii) the alleged motives for the crime, such as love and jealousy seen in (1) and (2); (iv) the dynamics of the violence itself. Building upon Fairclough's (1995: 4) assumption that media 'decide what to include, what to exclude, and what to 'foreground' and what to 'background'', in her monography on gender, discourse, and ideology in Italian, Formato (2019: Ch. 5) quantitatively analysed 331 newspaper articles published between 2013 and 2016. Using Sketch Engine (Kilgariff, 2012), she extracted the statistically most frequent terms in this corpus, the statistically relevant collocations of *gelosia* 'jealousy', *raptus, ennesimo* 'umpteenth', and *nuovo* 'new', the key terms in headlines, and the frequencies of victim-related lexemes relative to those of perpetrator-related lexemes. Formato (2019) concluded that the news reports included in her study focused on victims rather than on perpetrators. In the rare cases when perpetrators were foregrounded, this emphasis was selected to highlight their emotions or the general dynamics of the couple's relationship.

In our study, we have proceeded from the same starting point as Formato (2019): namely, Fairclough's (1995: 4) assumption that media narrate events from specific and sometimes biased vantage points. In contrast to Formato (2019), however, we opted to focus on *covert* textual abuses perpetrated by the writers choosing certain syntactic constructions over others. In particular, we quantitatively and qualitatively analysed argument structure constructions, such as active transitives, passives, anticausatives, reflexives, causatives, and nominalizations. These, on the one hand, favour perpetrators' backgrounding and suppression—ultimately diminishing their responsibility—and, conversely, favour emphasizing and foregrounding the responsibility of victims. Thus, our paper expands research into this topic by taking a quantitative approach focusing on Italian argument structure constructions.

This paper is structured as follows. Section 2 introduces our theoretical framework. In Sect. 3, the data and the methodology used for the analysis are presented. Section 4 reports the results of the analysis focusing both on the constructions that allow the backgrounding or suppression of the Agent (Sect. 4.1) and on those that foreground the Agent (Sect. 4.2). Section 5 discusses the implications of the results of the analysis. Section 6 offers some concluding remarks.

2   Theoretical Background

In accordance with the basic tenets of Construction Grammar (cf. e.g. Croft, 2001, 2012; Goldberg, 1995, 2006), we assume that grammatical constructions, such as argument structure constructions, are symbols in a Saussurean sense: constructions pair forms with meaning/function. Thus, lexicon and grammar constitute the two extreme poles of a *continuum* and differ merely in their degree of abstraction. As Goldberg (1995: 3) puts it, in a language, 'argument structure constructions are a special subclass of constructions that provides the basic means of clausal expression'. Discourse analysts also argue for the basicness of transitivity and argument structure constructions for humans' representation and understanding of events. As Fowler (1991: 71) puts it, 'transitivity is the foundation of representation: it is the way the clause is used to analyze events and situations as being of certain types' (Fowler, 1991: 71;

see also Van Dijk, 2008b). Thus, while choosing among different transitivity options, media make discursive choices which are meaningful from an ideological standpoint.

In the next subsections, we introduce the components needed to describe the constructional meanings/functions (Sect. 2.1). Then, we provide details concerning the meanings associated with each construction considered (Sect. 2.2) and finally, we look at their discursive effects (Sect. 2.3).

2.1 The Components of Argument Structure Constructions

In this paper, we describe the meanings of argument structure constructions and participants in the events that such constructions denote in terms of semantic roles. In what follows, we limit ourselves to summarizing and briefly defining the semantic roles relevant for the topics of the paper; for an updated discussion and a list of semantic roles, we refer to Kittilä, Västi, and Ylikoski (2011) and to Luraghi and Narrog (2014).

In a sentence such as *Luke sings*, the sole participant involved in the event of singing can be labelled in terms of semantic roles as an *Agent*, that is, an entity that causes and performs an action. Agents typically exercise a force over another entity, designated the Patient, and are characterized by intentionality and control. In a sentence such as ***Luke** eats an apple*, in which two participants are involved, *Luke* is the Agent whereas *an apple* is the Patient. The *Patient* role is played by the entity that undergoes a change of state performed by an Agent. Patients' defining feature is their degree of affectedness. In the preceding example, *Luke eats an apple*, the Patient *apple* is maximally affected by Luke eating it, as the apple goes from a state of being into a state of non-being. In GBV events, we expect the semantic role of Agent to be played by the perpetrator of the crime, and the semantic role of Patient to be played by the victim.

Two other semantic roles important for the description of violent events are the *Experiencer* and the *Stimulus*. These are two inverted roles:

Experiencer is the semantic role of the usually animate entity that experiences a physical or a psychological process (***Luke*** *is in love with Claire*) triggered by another entity or event, which is the Stimulus (*Luke is in love* ***with Claire***).

2.2   The Meanings Associated with Argument Structure Constructions

After defining the semantic components relevant for describing the participants in a GBV event, we go on to detail the abstract schemes underlying the argument structure constructions that represent those events (if not otherwise specified the abstract schemes are taken from the WALS online: https://wals.info).

Returning to the example *Luke sings*, this sentence instantiates an *intransitive construction*, that is, a construction in which a volitional Agent (*Luke*) performs an action (that of *singing*). The intransitive construction itself carries meaning, specifically, the just-outlined abstract scheme. Crucially, the abstract scheme of any construction can be filled by different verbs, which are, however, expected to be semantically consistent with the constructional abstract scheme (for a pioneering work on verb classes in English, see Levin, 1993).

The typical *transitive construction* portrays a situation in which a volitional Agent instigates an event that changes the state of affairs and affects a non-volitional Patient, as in *Luke* (Agent) *eats an apple* (Patient) discussed in Sect. 2.1. However, not all transitive verbs instantiating the transitive construction denote events whose participants can be described as Agents and Patients. For example, in *Luke loves Claire, Luke* is an Experiencer, whereas *Claire* is a Stimulus. In *Claire calls Luke*, instead, *Claire* indeed is an Agent, in that she voluntarily performs the action of calling *Luke*; however, Luke is not a Patient, as he does not undergo any change of state for being called by *Claire*. Thus, even transitive constructions can feature different degrees of transitivity (Hopper & Thompson, 1980). The extent of transitivity depends on the meaning of verbs, e.g. consumption (*eat*), emotion (*love*), communication (*call*) verbs, which instantiate the construction: verbs can be more or less agentive, based on the extent to which the first participant in subject position exercises voli-tion and control and the second participant in object position is affected by the event (Levin, 1993).

The *passive construction* indicates a situation in which a non-volitional Patient undergoes a change in their state of affairs and/or is affected by an event instigated by a volitional Agent. Crucially, the subject of the active transitive sentence becomes a non-obligatory oblique phrase in the passive, as in *An apple is eaten **by Luke***, or is omitted, as in *An apple is eaten Ø*, whereas the object of the active transitive becomes the subject of the passive. Thus, the passive construction results in Agent's demotion and in Patient's promotion (on the consequences of this, cf. Section 2.3).

As in the passive, in the situation denoted by an *anticausative construc-tion*, the subject is typically a Patient and not an Agent, as in the active transitive. In contrast to the passive construction, however, the anticausative does not entail any oblique or covert Agent: the event is simply depicted as being brought about spontaneously without the involvement of an Agent (Croft, 2012: 256). This difference can be appreciated by comparing the sentences *Chiara broke the vase* (active transitive), *The vase was broken (by Chiara)* (passive), and *The vase broke (by itself)* (anticausative). Certain events are very likely to be represented by means of the anticausative construction, typically weathering (*A storm has unleashed*) and diseases (*The disease has unfortunately worsened*), that is, events for which it is difficult to identify an agent directly responsible (Levin, 1993).

The *causative construction* denotes a complex situation comprising two sub-events: (i) the causing event, in which the causer (Agent) initiates something; (ii) the caused event, in which the causee carries out an action, or undergoes a change of state as a result of the causer's action. In a sentence such as *Erica makes **Chiara** fall*, the causee, *Chiara*, is a Patient, as she certainly falls with no intention. In *Erica makes **Chiara** learn Russian*, instead, *Chiara*, the causee, can also play the role of an Agent, in case she is willing to learn Russian and put some effort into doing so. In the *reflexive construction*, event-participants—usually, Agents—act on themselves: they are simultaneously the initiators and the endpoints of the denoted events (Croft, 2012: 236). See the differ-ence between the sentences *Chiara nominates Erica* vs. *Chiara nominates* *herself*: in the former, the endpoint of the event of nominating is Erica; in the latter, it is Chiara.

Finally, through nominalizations, verbs, typically representing events in terms of processes or actions, are reclassified as nouns, which customarily represent events in terms of objects and entities, that is, as 'reified processes' (Dunnmire, 2007; cf. also Billig, 2008a, 2008b; Fairclough, 2008; Martin, 2008; van Dijk, 2008a). Constructions with nominalizations, such as *running* or *destruction,* may contain modifiers referring to the participants in the event designated by the head nominalization, such as **Claire**'s *running* or *the destruction* **of the building**. Note that in **Claire**'s *running*, Chiara is the Agent in the action of running, while in *the destruction* **of the building**, *the building* is the Patient of the action of destroying. Nominalizations possess an inherent mystifying power (e.g. Fowler, 1991), which is explained by means of the following examples: *Departures have caused a lot of traffic jams.* By using the nominalization *departures* without any modifying noun with it, the actual people, (Agents) who voluntarily start their cars and end up causing said traffic jams, are consciously or unconsciously concealed.

2.3   The Discursive Effects of Argument Structure Constructions

Construction Grammar assumes constructions to be stored as such in the mental lexicon, that is, as pairs of forms and meanings. Construction Grammar is a functionalist model of language and thus aims to describe the language users' linguistic knowledge in a psychologically satisfying way. Indeed, a body of psycholinguistic studies has shown that the different abstract schemes associated with different argument structure constructions do not describe events in the same way, but rather produce focus-changing and other types of effects upon the addresses. With the passive construction in particular, for example, it has been demonstrated that its selection places emphasis on the object, rather than the subject, of the corresponding active sentence (Clark, 1965, 1976; Clark, & Begun, 1968; Johnson-Laird, 1968, 1977; Tannenbaum, & Williams, 1968; Turner, & Rommetveit, 1968). Put another way, verb voice biases addressees towards seeing the subject or the object of a sentence as the primary actor (Huttenlocher, Eisenberg, & Strauss, 1968; see also Rueschemeyer, & Gaskell 2018: ch. 22 with references therein).

Crucially, these psycholinguistic effects can be more or less consciously manipulated in media discourse to diminish GBV perpetrators' responsibility for the crime. The concrete mechanisms leading to this are summarized by Tranchese and Zollo (2013) among others. First, in passive and anticausative constructions, and in nominalizations, there is frequently neither direct reference to the Agent, which is supposedly co-referent with the GBV perpetrator. His responsibility is thus diminished by *suppression*. Second, in subjectless active, passive, anticausative and nominalization constructions, the perpetrator's responsibility is hidden by *backgrounding*: the Agent-perpetrator is not mentioned in relation to the crime, but is mentioned elsewhere in the text or defocused. Third, perpetrators can be relieved of their responsibility by *eventuation*. This is the case when anticausative and nominalization constructions are used, where the event—the crime in this context—is depicted as something that occurs spontaneously, without anyone voluntarily, actively initiating it. It follows that the active and reflexive constructions are the only argument structure constructions in which the Agent-perpetrator is foregrounded as it logically should be, given the dynamics of the event described in the newspaper articles in the corpus.

Previous studies of argument structure constructions relating to GBV have investigated languages other than Italian: Henley, Miller, and Beazley (1995) carried out a quantitative corpus- and psycholinguistic study of the usage and perception of passive voice in US media reports of GBV; Bohner (2001) performed a psycholinguistic experiment on German native speakers and investigated the usage of passive voice in reporting sexual assaults.

3   Data and Methods

For the present study, we compiled an *ad hoc* corpus consisting of 40 articles reporting on GBV events and published in four local daily Italian newspapers from 2017 to 2019. Our data comes from two local daily newspapers published in Northern Italy, *L'Eco di Bergamo*[5] (EB) and *La Provincia Pavese*[6] (PP), and two local daily newspapers published in Central or Southern Italy, *Corriere Adriatico*[7] (CA) and *Gazzetta del Sud*[8] (GS). Specifically, we selected 10 articles from each newspaper chosen for this study. The articles were collected using search words such as *femminicidio* 'femicide', *violenza contro le donne* 'violence against women', or *violenza di genere* 'gender-based violence'. It is important to point out that we considered only those cases of GBV in which the perpetrator has been definitely identified and his responsibility has been verified.

We focused on all verbs and nouns denoting GBV events in which the victim and the perpetrator were involved, even if not linguistically expressed. Thus, we omitted events in which the victim or the perpetrator interacted with other participants, such as the victim's relatives or police officers. We used *UAM Corpus Tool* (http://www.corpustool.com/) to annotate the argument structure of each verb or noun denoting GBV events. This tool was chosen because it allows us to build our own annotation scheme appropriate for addressing specific research questions. Our annotation scheme permitted us to annotate the argument structure of verbs or nouns and simultaneously keep track of other relevant contextual information in the description of the GBV event. Moreover, *UAM Corpus Tool* automatically outputs a quantitative and statistical analysis of the annotated data.

For each event, we manually annotated the following linguistic features: (a) nominal or verbal construction; (b) if verbal, which construction was used to represent the event (i.e. active, passive,

---

[5] *L'Eco di Bergamo* is the main newspaper of the province of Bergamo (Lombardy) and is one of the local Italian newspapers with the highest circulation in Northern Italy. From 2017 to 2019, it had a daily circulation (printed or online) between 33,000 and 38,000 copies (http://www.adsnotizie.it).

[6] *La Provincia Pavese* is the main local newspaper in the province of Pavia (Lombardy). In 2017, *La Provincia Pavese* had a circulation (printed or online) of 13,000 copies, that decreased to 10,000 copies in 2019 (http://www.adsnotizie.it).

[7] *Corriere Adriatico* is published in the Marche region. From 2017 to 2019, it had a circulation (printed or online) ranging from 12,000 to15,000 copies (http://www.adsnotizie.it).

[8] *Gazzetta del sud* is published in Messina (Sicily) and is one of the main local newspapers in Calabria and Sicily. In the period 2017-2019, *Gazzetta del Sud* had a circulation (printed or online) between 17,000 and 23,000 copies (http://www.adsnotizie.it).

causative, anticausative, reflexive); (c) linguistic overt expression or omission of the two participants (victim and perpetrator); d) features denoting the two participants (i.e. age, marital status, gender, nationality, etc.); (e) semantic role of the two participants (Agent, Patient, etc.); (f) occurrence of another participant and their semantic role. The total number of analysed constructions was 768.

4   The Analysis of Argument Structure Constructions

As noted in Sect. 2, the argument structure construction chosen to denote an event can affect the representation of the event itself. For this reason, we analyse here the constructions used to represent the GBV events, and we discuss them both quantitatively and qualitatively.

Table 1 shows that within our sample, active constructions were the most frequent (46.2%), followed by nominalizations (36.8%) and passive constructions (8.8%). Other less frequent but still interesting constructions were the anticausative (4.2%), the reflexive (2.8%), and the causative (0.9%). As mentioned in Sect. 2, the active construction describes an event in which a volitional Agent, and supposedly the perpetrator, brings about an action affecting a non-volitional Patient, and supposedly the victim. For this reason, it is not surprising that active was found to be the most frequent construction used to represent GBV events.

Table 1 Constructions used to represent GBV event in our corpus

Constructions	Raw frequency	%
Active	355	46.2
Nominalization	283	36.8
Passive	68	8.8
Anticausative	33	4.2
Reflexive	22	2.8
Causative	7	0.9
Total	768	

Table 2 Constructions that foreground or background/suppress the agent

	Constructions	Raw frequency	%
Agent foregrounded	Active+Causative+Reflexive	384	50
Agent backgrounded/suppressed	Nominalizations+Passive+Anticausative	384	50

In order to get quantitative linguistic clues to evaluate the degree of responsibility ascribed to the Agent, we compared the frequency of constructions that allow Agent promotion, i.e. active, causative and reflexive constructions, to the frequency of constructions that allow the Agent backgrounding or suppression, i.e. nominalizations, and passive and anticausative constructions (Table 2).

Table 2 shows that only in half of the constructions was the Agent foregrounded, while in the other half the Agent was backgrounded or suppressed. Since we expect the perpetrator to be the Agent of the event, it is sobering to note that the responsibility for the violence was assigned to the perpetrator only in 50% of cases. This percentage is both puzzling and troubling, especially if we consider that our corpus contained only articles reporting on GBV events in which the guilt of the perpetrator had been verified (Sect. 3). In the next subsections (4.1–4.2), we present additional quantitative data and a qualitative analysis for each construction contained in Tables 1 and 2.

4.1 Constructions with Backgrounded or Suppressed Agent: Quantitative and Qualitative Analysis

In this section, we focus on the constructions in which the Agent is backgrounded or suppressed, i.e. passives, anticausatives and nominalizations. It is important to analyze these constructions because their use in GBV discourse can shape a misleading representation of the events and diminish the Agent's responsibility. Table 3 shows the data concerning the passive construction.

We can observe that the role of Patient, foregrounded in passive constructions, was predominantly played by the victim (75%), while the

Table 3 Data concerning the passive construction

Passive 68 events (8.8%)	Agent	Patient	Occurrence in passive events
Victim	2 (2.9%)	51 (75%)	56 (82.3%)
Perpetrator	19 (27.9%)	1 (1.4%)	22 (32.3%)

perpetrator had the role of Agent, the backgrounded participant, only in 27.9% of passive events (Table 3). An example of passive construction is shown in (3):

(3) **Picchiata** brutalmente _dal fidanzato_ all'alba del primo dell'anno. (CA, Jan 2019) '[She was] brutally **hit** by [her] boyfriend at the dawn of the first day of the year.'

In (3), the passive past participle _picchiata_ 'hit' denotes an event in which the victim is the Patient, while the perpetrator is the Agent, defocused and coded as an oblique argument (_dal fidanzato_ 'by [her] boyfriend'). Table 3 further shows that the perpetrator was linguistically expressed in only 32.3% of passive events. Thus, the perpetrator was either a backgrounded Agent (27.9%) or, as in example (4), omitted in 67.7% of passive events.

(4) Lo scorso luglio _la donna_ **era stata scaraventata** a terra, al culmine di un violento litigio (...). (EB, Nov 2018) 'Last July, the woman **was thrown** to the ground at the height of a violent argument.'

In example (4), the passive construction places the Patient, _la donna_ 'the woman', i.e., the victim, in subject position, while there is no reference to the Agent of the verb _scaraventare_ 'throw', i.e., the perpetrator. Interestingly enough, in five passive events, participants other than the perpetrator were coded as Agents. This is exemplified in (5):

(5) L'infermiera **è stata colpita** _da un pugno_ che le ha fratturato il setto nasale. (PP, Jan 2019) 'The nurse **was hit** by a punch that fractured her nasal septum.'

The occurrence of another participant in the role of Agent causes a further diminishing of the perpetrator's responsibility: he is not only omitted, but his responsibilities are ascribed to someone or something else, for example *il pugno* 'the punch' in (5). The latter participant is further understood to have been able to initiate the event of *fratturare il setto nasale* 'fracture her nasal septum' in (5). Thus, in passive constructions, it is safe to conclude that the focus was more on victims than on perpetrators.

Nominalizations were the second most frequent constructions in our corpus (36.8% of events) and, much like anticausatives, they allow the representation of an action, performed by a volitional Agent in reality, as an involuntary event with obfuscated agency (Tranchese and Zollo, 2013: 149). This is the process that in Sect. 2 we called eventuation.

(6) *L'**aggressione** si è verificata, l'altra notte verso le due, in viale Sicilia.* (PP, Dec 2017) 'The **assault** occurred last night around 2 am in Viale Sicilia.'

In example (6), the noun *aggressione* 'assault', in contrast to the corresponding verb *aggredire* 'assault', depicts the GBV event omitting the participants (see more on this example below). As shown in Table 4, in the vast majority of nominalizations (80.9%) both the victim and the perpetrator were suppressed. However, overall, the victim (15.1%) was mentioned more frequently than the perpetrator (9.1%).

It is interesting to note that, in the 8 instances in which both participants were expressed (15 occurrences), the nominalization denoted an asymmetrical event, such as *danneggiamento* 'damage' and *aggressione* 'aggression, assault' (see example (7)), in which two asymmetrical participants play a role: an Agent-perpetrator and a Patient-victim.

Table 4 Data concerning the nominalization construction

Nominalization 283 events (36.8%)	No victim, no perpetrator	Victim only	Perpetrator only	Victim, perpetrator
	229 (80.9%)	28 (9.8%)	11 (3.8%)	15 (5.3%)

(7) *(...) nel 2008 era stata <u>vittima</u> di una violenta **aggressione** da parte del suo ex compagno.* (PP, Dec 2017) 'In 2008, [she] was <u>victim</u> of a violent **assault** by <u>her former partner.</u>'

In contrast, in 7/15 occurrences, the nominalization denoted a symmetrical or reciprocal relation, such as *lite/litigio* 'fight, argument' in (8), in which the two participants each play the same semantic role.

(8) *Sembra che il tutto sia avvenuto al culmine dell'ennesimo **litigio** <u>tra i due coniugi.</u>* (CA, Feb 2018) 'It seems that everything happened at the height of another **fight** <u>between the two spouses.</u>'

In (8), the noun *litigio* 'fight' depicts an event in which the participants are co-Agents: the victim and the perpetrator are put on the same level and equally share responsibility in the event. In the overall picture of GBV events culminating in femicides, this kind of representation is misleading, as it diminishes the perpetrator's responsibility and instead attributes equal responsibility to the victim.

Returning to example (6), we note that, in addition to nominalization, the anticausative construction *si è verificata* 'occurred' reinforces the eventuation of the violent act. Anticausatives, such as verbs of occurrence (*verificarsi* 'occur') and change of state verbs (*scatenarsi* 'break out', *aggravarsi* 'aggravate, worsen', *peggiorare* 'worsen'), usually denote spontaneous events (Sect. 2). Although anticausatives were fairly rare in our corpus (4.2% of events), their use sheds light on the representation of the GBV events, because, in the majority of cases (87.7%) the perpetrator was not mentioned, as we see in Table 5.

In anticausative constructions, the subject position can be filled by nominalizations (*aggressione* 'assault' in (6) above), generic nouns (*fatti* 'facts' in (9)), or even emotions (*furia* 'fury' in (10)).

Table 5 Data concerning the anticausative construction

Anticausative 33 events (4.2%)	No victim, no perpetrator	Victim only	Perpetrator only	Victim + perpetrator
	23 (69.6%)	6 (18.1%)	2 (6%)	2 (6%)

(9) *I fatti **si sono verificati** a Caravaggio negli ultimi 3 anni circa (…).* (EB, Oct 2018) 'The facts **occurred** in Caravaggio over the last 3 years, approximately (…).'

(10) *La furia omicida **si è scatenata** nel pomeriggio in un appartamento di Pietra Ligure.* (GS, Mar 2017) 'The murderous fury **broke out** in the afternoon in an apartment in Pietra Ligure.'

Although an act of aggression or a femicide logically requires an agent to be achieved, examples (6), (9), and (10) show that anticausatives represent the violence as a spontaneous event that 'occurs' or 'breaks out' with no mention of a voluntary initiator.

4.2 Constructions with Foregrounded Agent: Quantitative and Qualitative Analysis

In this section, we analyse in detail GBV events represented by constructions foregrounding the Agent, i.e. the actives, the causatives and the reflexives.

In Tables 6 and 7, the results concerning the reflexive and the causative constructions are summarized. Although not very frequent in the corpus, these two constructions put the focus on the Agent, which usually coincided with the perpetrator. When the Agent was the perpetrator, the verbs denoted aggression, as in the cases of *scagliarsi* '(lit.) launch oneself against' and *far cadere* 'make someone fall'. Conversely, in those rare cases in which the Agent was the victim, the verbs denoted a condition of

Table 6 Data concerning the reflexive construction

Reflexive 22 events (2.8%)		Agent	Patient
	Victim	9 (40%)	0
	Perpetrator	13 (59%)	0

Table 7 Data concerning the causative construction

Causative 7 events (0.9%)		Agent	Patient
	Victim	1 (14.2%)	4 (57.1%)
	Perpetrator	5 (71.4%)	1 (14.2%)

Table 8   Data concerning the active construction

Active 355 events (46.2%)		Agent	Patient
	Victim	59 (16.6%)	154 (43.3%)
	Perpetrator	255 (71.8%)	14 (3.9%)

submission and/or coercion, such as *difendersi* 'defend oneself', *divincolarsi* 'wiggle out of something', and *far salire (forzatamente in casa)* 'force (someone) to go into (the house)'.

We can now look at the results concerning active constructions (Table 8). These, the most numerous in the corpus, foreground the Agent and his responsibility.

Table 8 shows that, as expected, the perpetrator played the role of Agent in the majority of active events (71.8%), while the victim mainly was represented by the Patient (43.3%). When the perpetrator was the Agent, the verbs occurring in the active construction, such as *picchiare* 'beat', *aggredire* 'assault/attack', *colpire* 'hit', *costringere* 'force/obligate', showed a high degree of transitivity: this indicates that the Agent's action markedly affected the Patient (see example (11)). In sharp contrast, in those case in which the role of Agent was played by the victim (16.6% of active constructions), the degree of agentivity was lower, as was the degree of affectedness of the Patient (Sect. 2). In most cases, the victim was the Agent of communication verbs, such as *denunciare* 'report' (cf. example (12)), *accusare* 'accuse', and *urlare* 'scream'.

(11) *Lo straniero giovedì scorso* **ha picchiato** *selvaggiamente* la compagna, *un'ucraina 35enne.* (EB, Sept 2017) 'Last Thursday, the foreign man wildly **beat** his partner, a 35-year-old Ukrainian (woman).'

(12) *La donna l'* **ha denunciato** *dopo la fine della relazione.* (PP, July 2018) 'The woman **sued** him after the relationship ended.'

Undoubtedly, the active construction is the one that best matches the reality of the violent event, as it foregrounds the Agent and directly assigns responsibility to him.

5   Discussion

In this section, we further develop our analysis and ultimately argue that the representation of GBV events is even more biased than our evidence from Sect. 4 suggests. First, we consider the extent to which factors other than the basic representation of an event can play a role in the selection of certain constructions over others. Second, we show that quantitative data from Sect. 4 is actually misleading with regard to the perpetrator's actual foregrounding, due to a mismatch between linguistic Agents and actual perpetrators. Third, even in constructions which foreground perpetrators, other details framing the GBV event can diminish perpetrators' responsibility.

As seen above (Sect. 4.2), the transitive active construction in principle is fair in foregrounding the Agent and attributing responsibility to him in the event. However, a deeper analysis shows that, even in active constructions, the Agent-perpetrator can be backgrounded and thus relieved of his responsibility. Indeed, in 65.8% of active constructions, the reference to the perpetrator is via anaphora, as shown in Table 9 and exemplified in (13) and (14).

(13) *Sempre a ottobre l'uomo aveva anche cercato di soffocare la vittima,* **sferrandole** *una testata in pieno volto e* **procurandole** *così una frattura scomposta alle ossa nasali.* (EB, Nov 2018) 'In October the man had also tried to suffocate the victim, **head-butting her** in the face and **causing** a compound fracture of her nasal bones.'

(14) **Picchia** *e* **minaccia** *convivente per anni.* (Headline, EB, Nov 2018) '[He] **hits** and **threatens** the cohabitant for years.'

Table 9 Anaphoric and non-anaphoric reference to participants in active constructions

Active 355 events (46.2%)	Anaphoric	Non-Anaphoric	Total
Agent perpetrator	168 (65.8%)	87 (34.1%)	255
Agent victim	21 (35.5%)	38 (64.4%)	59

An anaphoric construction is arguably chosen for reasons of text cohesion in (13), in which two coordinated gerunds occur whose omitted subject is co-referent with the subject of the main verb, i.e., *l'uomo* 'the man'. By contrast, in (14) the null subject cannot simply result from strategies of textual cohesion: example (14) is taken from a headline, in which reference to previously mentioned participants is not possible. In any case, whether for textual cohesion or not, the omission of the Agent-perpetrator favours its backgrounding in discourse.

A similar argument can be made for the passive constructions discussed in Sect. 4.1: the occurrence of a passive in discourse, especially after an active construction, can result from applying principles of textual cohesion or from inherent features of the journalistic style (Cresti, 1999; De Cesare, 2007; Sansò, 2003, 2006). However, it is interesting to observe that the passive construction is frequently used in headlines (see examples (15)–(18)), for which no textual cohesion motives can be invoked.

(15) *Marisa, uccisa con una coltellata al cuore* (EB, Nov 2019) 'Marisa, killed with a stab wound to the heart.'

(16) *Segregata e violentata per un anno, un arresto* (GS, May 2018) 'Isolated and raped for one year, one arrest.'

(17) *Badante uccisa e gettata nel fiume* (PP, Feb 2018) 'Carer killed and dumped in the river'

(18) *Pesaro, l'omicidio è premeditato: Maria uccisa dal marito dopo l'ennesimo "no"* (CA, Aug 2019) 'Pesaro, the murder is premeditated: Maria killed by her husband after the umpteenth "no"'

What is crucial is that the reasons for the authorial selection of certain constructions over others (e.g. textual cohesion, journalistic genre, event representation) do not change their deliberate or accidental impact on the readers' perceptions: the omission of the Agent-perpetrator in active and passive constructions has the effect of shifting focus from the responsible perpetrator of the GBV event to the victim of it.

Moreover, the analysis put forward in Sect. 4 does not take into account the fact that a mismatch exists between the semantic role of Agent in the linguistic construction and the perpetrator of the GBV event in reality. The data from Table 2 above indicates that only 50% of

GBV events tagged in our corpus are described by means of constructions that foreground the Agent. However, what Table 2 data cannot convey is the fact that the participant playing the semantic role of Agent in the construction is not always the actual initiator of the violence in reality, i.e. the perpetrator. Thus, in order to evaluate the degree of responsibility attributed to the actual perpetrator in different argument structure constructions, we compared three different GBV event representations: (i) constructions with foregrounded Agent and in which—crucially—it is the perpetrator playing the role of Agent; (ii) constructions in which the perpetrator is expressed but backgrounded, owing to the construction itself or the fact that the perpetrator does not act in the role of Agent in the construction; c) constructions with suppression of the perpetrator as Agent of the violence. These results are displayed in Table 10.

Table 10 shows that the perpetrator not only is backgrounded in 21% of cases, but even more telling, in the majority of events (42%), is entirely omitted. As a result, in only 37% of events are the perpetrator and his responsibility fully foregrounded by means of active, causative or reflexive constructions in which he is represented by the semantic role of Agent.

Finally, even in this relatively small percentage of constructions in which the perpetrator is foregrounded, his responsibility can be mitigated in other ways (cf. Abis, & Orrù, 2016; Formato, 2019). For example, the GBV event can be framed in such ways as to foreground the role of his

Table 10 Constructions which focus or defocus the perpetrator

	Construction	Raw frequency (%)
Perpetrator foregrounded	Active (perpetrator_Agent), causative (perpetrator_Agent), reflexive (perpetrator_Agent)	272 (37%)
Perpetrator backgrounded (Perpetrator expressed)	Passives, anticausatives, nominalizations, actives (perpetrator_non-Agent), reflexives (victim_Agent), causative (victim_Agent)	156 (21%)
Perpetrator suppression (Perpetrator not expressed)	Passives, anticausatives, nominalizations	316 (42%)

altered mental state (19) or the victim's co-responsibility (20) in creating the tense conditions that allegedly led to the femicide.

(19) *L'uomo era in preda ad un raptus e **ha anche cercato di spogliarla.*** (PP, Jun 2018) 'The man was in the throes of rapture and **he also tried to undress her.**'

(20) *L'uomo avrebbe raccontato che al culmine di una violenta lite **ha accoltellato e ucciso la consorte.*** (CA, Feb 2019) 'The man allegedly said that at the height of a violent quarrel **he stabbed and killed his wife.**'

These frames shift the perpetrator's responsibility to his emotions/uncontrollable passions and to the couple's dynamics.

6   Conclusions

In this paper, we investigated how GBV events and their two main participants, i.e., the victim and the perpetrator, are represented in four local Italian newspapers. Specifically, we showed that argument structure plays a critical role in shaping GBV events in discourse, and that constructional choices can favour particular, sometimes misleading, interpretations of the events by foregrounding, backgrounding or suppressing participants.

Our analysis of constructions such as passives, nominalizations, and anticausatives showed that the perpetrator's responsibility is diminished by Agent backgrounding or suppression and by presenting the violent event as spontaneous, i.e. by eventuation. A more detailed analysis of passive constructions revealed that the perpetrator is not only represented as a backgrounded Agent but is in most cases (67.7%) suppressed. Moreover, it was observed that the passive construction cannot be explained merely by invoking the need for textual cohesion, as it is used in headline as well as in the body of the articles. Nominalizations, the second most frequent construction examined in the corpus, suppressed the perpetrator in the 90.7% of events; additionally, nominalizations that refer to symmetrical relations balanced the responsibility of victim and perpetrator and consequently, diminished the perpetrator's primary responsibility by focusing on the victim's co-responsibility.

As we expected, the active construction was the most frequent in the corpus and ascribed to the foregrounded Agent, mainly the perpetrator (71%), full responsibility for the action expressed by the verb. However, a closer analysis revealed that anaphora was used to refer to the perpetrator as the Agent in 65.8% of active events. Also, even when active constructions were used to describe the event, other contextual elements, such as references to couple dynamics or altered mental states, were sometimes employed with the effect of diminishing perpetrator's responsibility.

Overall, our analysis of argument structure constructions confirmed that GBV reports mainly focus on victims as responsible parties, while perpetrators are backgrounded and relieved from their full share of responsibility.

References

Abis, S., & Orrù, P. (2016). Il femminicidio nella stampa italiana: un'indagine linguistica. *Gender/Sexuality/Italy, 3,* 18–33.

Benwell, B. (2007). New sexism? Readers' responses to the use of irony in men's magazines. *Journalism Studies, 8*(4), 539–549.

Billig, M. (2008a). The language of critical discourse analysis: The case of nominalization. *Discourse & Society, 19*(6), 783–800.

Billig, M. (2008b). Nominalizing and de-nominalizing: A reply. *Discourse & Society, 19*(6), 829–841.

Bohner, G. (2001). Writing about rape: Use of the passive voice and other distancing text features as an expression of perceived responsibility of the victim. *British Journal of Social Psychology, 40,* 515–529.

Clark, H. H. (1965). Some structural properties of simple active and passive sentences. *Journal of Verbal Learning and Verbal Behavior, 4,* 365–370.

Clark, H. H. (1976). *Semantics and comprehension.* Paris: Mouton.

Clark, H. H., & Begun, J. S. (1968). The use of syntax in understanding sentences. *British Journal of Psychology, 59,* 219–229.

Coates, L., & Wade, A. (2007). Language and violence: Analysis of four discursive operations. *Journal of Family Violence, 22,* 511–522.

Cresti, A. (1999). Il passivo in italiano. Occorrenze e funzioni nel parlato e nello scritto. *Romanische Forschungen, 111*(2), 161–177.

Croft, W. (2001). *Radical construction grammar*. Oxford: Oxford University Press.

Croft, W. (2012). *Verbs: Aspect and causal structure*. Oxford: Oxford University Press.

De Cesare, A.-M. (2007). Le funzioni del passivo agentivo. Tra sintassi, semantica e testualità. *Vox Romanica, 66,* 32–59.

Dunnmire, P. L. (2007). *Projecting the future through political discourse: The case of the Bush Doctrine*. Amsterdam: Benjamins.

Ehrlich, S. (2003). *Representing rape: Language and sexual consent*. London: Routledge.

Fagoaga, C. (1994). Comunicando violencia contra las mujeres. *Estudio Sobre El Mensaje Periodístico, 1,* 67–90.

Fairclough, N. (1989). *Language and power*. London: Longman.

Fairclough, N. (1995). *Media discourse*. London: Hodder Education.

Fairclough, N. (2008). The language of critical discourse analysis: Reply to Michael Billig. *Discourse & Society, 19*(6), 811–819.

Formato, F. (2019). *Gender, discourse and ideology in Italian*. Cham, Switzerland: Palgrave Macmillan.

Fowler, R. (1991). *Language in the news: Discourse and ideology in the press*. London: Routledge.

Goddard, C., & Saunders, B. J. (2000). The gender neglect and textual abuse of children in the print media. *Child Abuse Review, 9,* 37–48.

Goldberg, A. E. (1995). *Constructions: A construction grammar approach to argument structure*. Chicago: University of Chicago Press.

Goldberg, A. E. (2006). *Constructions at work: The nature of generalizations in language*. Oxford: Oxford University Press.

Graddoll, D., & Swan, J. (1989). *Gender voices*. Oxford: Blackwell.

Henley, N. M., Miller, M., & Beazley, J. A. (1995). Syntax, semantics, and sexual violence: Agency and the passive voice. *Journal of Language and Social Psychology, 14*(1/2), 60–84.

Hopper, P. J., & Thompson, A. A. (1980). Transitivity in grammar and discourse. *Language, 56*(2), 251–299.

Huttenlocher, J., Eisenberg, K., & Strauss, S. (1968). Comprehension: Relation between perceived actor and logical subject. *Journal of Verbal Learning and Verbal Behavior, 7,* 527–530.

Johnson, M. P. (1995). Patriarchal terrorism and common couple violence: Two forms of violence against women. *Journal of Marriage and Family, 57,* 283–294.

Johnson-Laird, P. N. (1968). The interpretation of the passive voice. *The Quarterly Journal of Experimental Psychology, 20*(1), 69–73.

Johnson-Laird, P. N. (1977). The passive paradox: A reply to Costermans and Hupet. *British Journal of Psychology, 68,* 113–116.

Karadole, C. (2012). Anti-violence centres and shelters in Italy: History and meaning of women's struggles against male violence. *Interdisciplinary Journal of Family Studies, 17*(2), 238–242.

Kilgariff, A. (2012). Getting to know your corpus. In P. Sojka, A. Horák, I. Kopeček, & K. Pala (Eds.), *Text, speech and dialogue: TSD 2012. Lecture notes in computer science, vol 7499* (pp. 3–15). Berlin: Springer.

Kittilä, S., Västi, K., & Ylikoski, J. (Eds.). (2011). *Case, animacy, and semantic roles.* Amsterdam: Benjamins.

Lakoff, R. (1973). Language and woman's place. *Language in Society, 2*(1), 45–79.

Lakoff, R. (1975). *Language and woman's place.* New York: Harper.

Lazar, M. (Ed.). (2005). *Feminist critical discourse analysis: Gender, power and ideology in discourse.* London: Palgrave Macmillan.

Levin, B. (1993). *English verb classes and alternations.* Chicago: University of Chicago Press.

Luraghi, S., & Narrog, H. (Eds.). (2014). *Perspectives on semantic roles.* Amsterdam: Benjamins.

Martin, J. R. (2008). Incongruent and proud: De-vilifying 'nominalization'. *Discourse & Society, 19*(6), 801–810.

Meyers, M. (1997). *News coverage of violence against women: Engendering blame.* London: Sage.

Mills, S. (2008). *Language and sexism.* Cambridge: Cambridge University Press.

Monckton-Smith, J. (2012). *Murder, gender and the media: Narratives of gendered love.* Basingstoke: Palgrave Macmillan.

O'Hara, S. (2012). Monsters, playboys, virgins and whores: Rape myths in the news media's coverage of sexual violence. *Language and Literature, 21*(3), 247–259.

Rueschemeyer, S.-A., & Gaskell, M. G. (2018). *The Oxford handbook of psycholinguistics.* Oxford: Oxford University Press.

Sansò, A. (2003). *Degrees of event elaboration: Passive constructions in Italian and Spanish.* Milano: Franco Angeli.

Sansò, A. (2006). Agent defocusing revisited: Passive and impersonal constructions in some European languages. In W. Abraham & L. Leisiö (Eds.), *Passivization and typology: Form and function* (pp. 232–273). Amsterdam: Benjamins.

Santaemilia, J., & Maruenda, S. (2014). The linguistic representation of gender violence in written media discourse: The term 'woman' in Spanish contemporary newspapers. *Journal of Language Aggression and Conflict, 2*(2), 249–273.

Schaeffer, J. D. (1990). *Sensus communis: Vico, Rhetoric and the limits of relativism.* Durham: Duke University Press.

Scott, J. C. (1990). *Domination and the arts of resistance.* New Haven, CT: Yale University Press.

Tannenbaum, P. H., & Williams, F. (1968). Generation of active and passive sentences as a function of subject or object focus. *Journal of Verbal Learning and Verbal Behavior, 7,* 246–250.

Tranchese, A., & Zollo, S. A. (2013). The construction of gender-based violence in the British printed and broadcast media. *Critical Approaches to Discourse Analysis Across Disciplines, 7*(1), 141–163.

Turner, E. A., & Rommetveit, R. (1968). Focus of attention in recall of active and passive sentences. *Journal of Verbal Learning and Verbal Behavior, 7,* 543–548.

Van Dijk, T. A. (2008a). Critical discourse analysis and nominalization: Problem or pseudproblem? *Discourse & Society, 19*(6), 821–828.

Van Dijk, T. A. (2008b). *Discourse and power.* New York: Palgrave Macmillan.

Williamson, J. (2003). Sexism with an alibi. *Eye* 48(12) [online]. http://www.eyemagazine.com/feature/article/retro-sexism-extract (accessed 20 July, 2019).

Wykes, M. (1995). Passion, marriage and murder. In R. P. Dobash, L. Noaks, & R. E. Dobash (Eds.), *Gender and crime* (pp. 49–76). Cardiff: University of Wales Press.

The Ethos of the Spokesperson: A Populist Attempt to Exploit Empathic Connections

Aurora Fragonara

1   Introduction

Populist speeches have recently emerged in the field of political discourses. According to many researchers, populism can be regarded as a fragmented or thin ideology (Engesser, Ernst, Esser, & Büchel, 2017; Kriesi, 2014), since it does not rely on a well-defined political programme.

Globally speaking, populist discourses draw on the "*us vs them*" opposition of points of view and believes (Ernst, Engesser, Büchel, & Blassnig, 2017). In this binary paradigm, *us* is generally identified with the national community (often referred to as "the people"), while the pronominal label *them* reunites all the opponents (often demonized as "enemies") of this national community. This categorization of the *them*-group is also applied to different social groups, according to

A. Fragonara (✉)
University of Bergamo and University of Milan, Bergamo/Milan, Italy
e-mail: aurora.fragonara@guest.unibg.it

© The Author(s), under exclusive license to Springer Nature   **145**
Switzerland AG 2021
P. Anesa and A. Fragonara (eds.), *Discourse Processes between Reason and Emotion*, Postdisciplinary Studies in Discourse,
https://doi.org/10.1007/978-3-030-70091-1_7

the contextual and communication purpose of the discourse. Populists' schematization of society identifies two main subcategories. The "others" to whom populist speakers are referring to can often be the immigrants (perceived as a threat for the social order or the welfare state of the country) or the *élite*, a designation that reunites several high social positions, such as politicians and experts in many fields (science or economics, for example). The discourses that revolve around the *them*-group are usually conceived to enhance indignation in order to discredit the government actions. As many studies have pointed out (see Krämer, 2017; Ernst et al., 2017), the mode and tone used are often violent, so that those discourses are often referred to as "hate speeches". This strategy consists merely in demonizing the opponents, blaming them for the poor or negative outcome of complex situations. Moreover, these discourses tend to simplify content, through loose formulations and vague lexical choices.

In rhetorical terms, this kind of discourse relies mainly on the *pars destruens,* since populist politicians generally tend to attack the government or blame the enemies (the *élites*, the migrants, EU) that undermine the people's well-being. A large part of this activity is also based on the presupposition that the elected politicians (the so-called *élite*) are not representing national interests.

However, even if these discourses, charged with hate and negative emotions, represent a large part of populists' communication strategy, the *us*-group is also taken into consideration, since it is the final target. The discursive strategies conceived to reach out to this group are aimed to direct their anger against the *them*-groups, as well as to define the position of the speaker in relation to the people and the *élite* (Krämer, 2017).

Indeed, this Manichean vision of society and of power relationships, which radically opposes the centre of power and the national will, insists also on the exceptionality of the image of the populist politician. Populist personalities present themselves as the counterpart of these *élites* as well as the true representatives of the people. They generally refer to themselves as outsiders, marginalized, and therefore hated by the establishment and banned from the political circles. This distancing strategy from the centre of the political power aims to identify a "common ground" where the speakers can easily target their audiences. By differentiating themselves from the other political parties, populist speakers manage to convey an impression of proximity with the masses. Traces of this mental frame can be found in their discourses, starting from the selection of particular topics, which accounts for a certain vision of the world.

However, this rigid divide of reality into groups inspires not only the topic selection for the political and public arena (as in the case of the "hate speech"), but orientates also the choice of the communication strategies, especially for the discursive construction of the speaker's identity. Since populist politicians tend and want to convey an image of proximity to the people, we can argue that they will try to show that they share some social background with the potential voters and that they are able to understand their needs.

The present study draws on the theoretical concepts (linguistics and psychological) of *ethos* (the image that the speakers convey of themselves in discourse), as it has been theorized in French-speaking countries, and empathy (the ability to adopt someone else's perspective in order to understand—and share—his/her vision of reality). The research has been carried out on a digital corpus: we have focused on the online discursive production via Twitter by two politicians often referred to as populists in their countries (Marine Le Pen and Nigel Farage). The analysis of these tweets has enabled us to identify some features of their speeches which are related to the image they aim to project of themselves in discourse and, consequentially, to the connection they wish to establish with their audiences.

The first section of our work defines the two concepts of *ethos* and empathy. The second section presents the corpus and points out the interest of applying the theoretical framework to the populist online communication via Twitter. The final section consists in the analysis of the data.

2   The Theoretical Framework

2.1   The Concept of *Ethos* and Its Relevance in Political Discourse

In order to study the construction of the self in the political communication of the so-called populist exponents, we apply a theoretical framework combining concepts from the French linguistics theory on *ethos* (Amossy, 2010; Charaudeau, 2014; Maingueneau, 2014) with studies on the discursive and textual construction of the point of view (Rabatel, 1998, 2017). The work by these French scholars develops the concept of discursive positioning into a theory of the *ethos*-in-discourse. According to Maingueneau and Amossy, the discursive *ethos* is the image a speaker builds (and conveys) of him/herself in discourse. The concept of *ethos* is nevertheless related to other concepts forming the overall discursive theory. *Ethos* is modelled not only with reference to the discourse positioning practice but it is also related and influenced by the discursive genre and the situation of communication: for example, doctors are likely to model the image they project of themselves according to the role they play during a consultation, which is also defined by the standard structure of this kind of interaction. Furthermore, specificity may be detected according to the specific situation in which the interaction takes place, for example, according to the age of the patient. In other words, the *ethos* is socially negotiated and the image that the speaker projects of him/herself is the result of the interactions carried out in a given context. Likewise, each subject enters the communicational exchange with a set of pre-constructed notional elements about the social identity of the interlocutor. In this regard, the interaction is meant to confirm or invalidate, totally or partially, the image they have.

As Amossy (2010) points out, the concept of *ethos* applied to political discourse derives from Aristotle' s work. According to Aristotle, the displayed *ethos* is crucial to a successful and persuasive communication. One of the key elements of this process is the concordance of the pre- or inner-*ethos* with the one expressed in discourse. Without this equation, the discourse is not convincing, since the speaker is perceived as false and untruthful.

In political discourse, especially in the electoral period, gaining trust is considered to be one of the main goals for a politician. Being trusted means that you can get elected and therefore enact your programme. However, becoming worthy of trust could be a quite complicated task, which requires the adoption of communication strategies and the construction of a specific *ethos*, in relation to the electoral programme, in order to persuade the citizens so that they cast a vote for the speaker's party.

Trust can indeed be gained in many ways, according to the image one decides to adopt. According to Patrick Charaudeau (2014), there are three main kinds of political *ethos*: the *ethos* of competence, the *ethos* of credibility and the *ethos* of identification. Most of the time, they are entangled. The *ethos* of competence aims to convey an image of seriousness and technical competence in handling different matters of the public life. The *ethos* of credibility reflects the correspondence between the public and the personal image of the politicians, and, therefore, between their declarations, their actions and their behaviours. Finally, the *ethos* of identification is the result of the psychological process that brings the audience ideally closer to the leader. It is based on the (perceived) belonging of the politician to the community of "common people", who trusts his/her as a leader. These three *ethé* are closely tied and co-occurrent in the process of consensus building. However, Charaudeau claims that in populist discourses the *ethos* of identification is the most prominent one. Populism being a "thin" ideology, populists tend to side with the population using the *pathos* leverage in their communication. In other words, they stimulate the sentimental triggers in the audience's minds. This strategy relies mainly on the emotional component of human nature. Therefore, the *ethos* of identification may be regarded as their main communicational asset, in order to build credibility.

As we have already pointed out, the construction of *ethos* can work simultaneously in two directions: from the speaker to the addressee and backwards. This means that the image the speakers aim to communicate about themselves has to be validated from the audience. The *ethos* of identity implicates a higher level of approbation, since it is characterized not only by the recognition of some qualities of the speaker (competence and credibility), but also by the inclusion of the speaker in the same social sphere of experience as the audience (the voters). In this sense, this kind of *ethos* is closely related to the concept of empathic connection and to the use that can be done in (political) discourses (Lakoff, 2008).

2.2   Empathy and Discourse

Empathy is commonly defined as the ability to put yourself in "someone else's shoes" (Pinotti, 2016), the ability to adopt someone else's perspective and reconstruct—by using our imagination—their feelings, thoughts and mindsets when going through a specific experience. Empathy can be regarded as a social ability proper to human beings and big apes (De Waal, 2010). Some studies have shown that empathic behaviours are rooted in our biological evolution, since they encourage pro-social actions and therefore grant the survival and continuity of the species (Berthoz & Jorland, 2004; Brunel & Cosnier, 2014).

Despite the underlying evolutionary reasons, which would suggest that empathy is quite spontaneous, this kind of behaviour is actually quite complex. It is based on the projective imaginative effort that the speakers make in order to reconstruct their addressees' vision of the world. The empathic process implies the assumption of different cognitive and enunciative postures. Empathy is based on a come-and-go process: firstly, the speaker reconstructs by projection the perspective angle of the addressee, then she/he repositions herself/himself by re-assuming their original discursive position. Every empathic decentralization is in fact a temporary mental state which requires the repositioning of the empathic subject in his/her own original mental state and perspective; otherwise, the result would be an emotional contagion, a state where the boundaries between the perceptions of the addresser and of the addressee are blurred and result in a total immersion and identification of the speaker in the situation of his/her counterpart (Decety, 2004, 2005).

In other words, the empathic process requires that the speaker is aware of his/her position towards a given event. Alterity is not completely obliterated and the maintenance of a certain distance actually facilitate the empathic attitude and its expression.

In discursive terms, empathic expression implies a shift between two different points of views which are related to two different positions. The effects, intentions and uses that the adoption of an empathic attitude can have on discursive practices are multiple and variable according to the context. In the case of populist discourses, we have already argued that politicians may attempt to convey an empathic impression in order to strengthen the *ethos* of identification. This attempt may be reached by specific linguistic features. In order to investigate these discursive strategies, we have looked into a corpus built from tweets of two politicians, perceived as populists in their countries: Marine Le Pen and Nigel Farage. In the following section, we provide a brief description of the digital corpus we have chosen, as well as of the methodology adopted.

3   The Corpus Presentation and Analysis

3.1   The Features of Twitter

The choice of social media discourses and the focus on Twitter are functional to the purposes of our investigation. It has been observed that, nowadays, social media are a new and powerful mean of communication for politicians. Social networks reunite the three concepts that are useful to political communication: they are pervasive, quick and interactive (Ernst et al., 2017, Krämer, 2017). These features enable the politicians to communicative effectively, to establish a certain image of him/herself and to incorporate the presence and the point of view of the potential voters in their speeches.

This interest for online communication is mainly due to the fact that social media have an increased power of diffusion: compared to traditional media (the press, television, for example), they have a great outreach in terms of potential addressees, also because they are supported by wide-spread devices such as laptops computers and smartphones. In this sense, they are quick and pervasive: communication through the Internet is faster and therefore enables to reach a larger amount of people in a shorter time compared to analogical media.

Concerning political communication, social media represent the optimal way to campaign, raise awareness and to spread one's idea. The Internet 2.0 has reshaped the interaction with the audience: social networks are often regarded as a useful way to get feedback from the audience, to grasp what are the people's orientation or feelings towards a specific topic or a given issue.

However, online communication—as every kind of communication—presents also some boundaries. They mainly consist in the genre specificities (Maingueneau, 2014) that codify the selection of subjects as well as the modes in which the content is expressed and spread across via devices in specific social contexts. Social media communication has also brought attention to the limits defined by the technological support which is used. The design of Networks 2.0, such as Facebook, Instagram and Twitter, prescribes a certain interaction between text and image (in the case of Instagram the presence of the image is even mandatory) and also limits the number of characters the speaker is allowed to use. The design of the technical support is part of the so-called ecology of the media (Peraya, 1998; Paveau, 2012, 2013; Strate, 2004)[1]: the set of technological features, social practices and cognitive frames that are related to the use of language. The interplay of the language with its material and social contexts means not only that the language can influence the context (that would be the case of the pragmatics approach) but also that the context shapes the message, even in its small and factual structures. In the case of Twitter, the limits set to the number of characters the addresser can use results in a careful selection of the content. Being populism a "thin" ideology, with a light conceptual expression, we can argue that the condensation of the message would rarely target rational argumentation and would be more likely to arise feelings and apply to emotions. The analysis of our corpus will look into this hypothesis and identify the salient linguistic structures.

---

[1]The concept of ecology, meaning the interaction between the external word and the human mind and body has been first theorised by cognitivist scientists (Bateson, 1980; Gibson, 1979; Hutchins, 1995). More recently, some French researchers have introduced this concept in the linguistic (Achard-Bayle & Paveau, 2012; Paveau, 2012, 2013) and semiotic fields (Mitropoulou & Pignier, 2014; Peraya, 1998). It should be noticed that the question of the role of the extralinguistic material was already present in the French-speaking research community, for example in Georges Kleiber's work (1997).

3.2   Methodology

The study compares four bilingual corpora. Two pilot corpora, established in 2016–2017, based on the tweets about Brexit (Farage) and presidential elections (Le Pen), and two current corpora (April–November 2020) on political and social domestic or international matters, such as the pandemic. We have adopted a mixed methodology (Guilbert, 2014), both quantitative and qualitative. The analysis of the two accounts has been carried out through Maxqda, a software specifically designed for this kind of analysis, which enables to tag and classify items presenting the same linguistic markers.

However, in order to understand the empathic use of discourse, a specific attention has been drawn to qualitative analysis. In the light of the definition we have provided above, empathy is, in fact, a phenomenon to be studied in context. This means that several enunciative and textual parameters have to be taken into account as well as their combination, in order to describe the intention of the sentences. In this respect, the quantitative analysis is here a preliminary step to the qualitative one: it is useful to get a general picture of the main linguistic markers.

Overall, we have analysed 281 tweets published on the two officials accounts. The selection of the tweets has been made following two criteria: the presence of the "*nous/we*" and its derivative forms. Among the tweets presenting these markers, we focused on the ones where the "*we/nous*" refer to the national communities, since they show the voluntary inclusion of the speaker in the common people's group. The tweets where the pronouns and their derivatives are referred to the sole political parties have been excluded. The other tweets that were not taken into account mainly consist in reposted messages and tweets attacking the government.

The following steps consisted in selecting all the tweets presenting the designation of an addressee, such as specific social groups. We have conducted a qualitative analysis drawing upon the framework conceptualized by Dominique Maingueneau on discourse positioning (1999, 2009, 2014), and by Alain Rabatel (1998, 2005, 2008, 2017) on the textual construction of points of view, the role of the enunciator (*énonciateur*) and the speaker (*locuteur*) as well as on the notion of indirect speech (Banfield, 1979). The articulation of the work by these authors, which revolves around the concept of enunciation, theorized by Benveniste (1966, 1974), has enabled us to identify the markers connected to the concept of empathy.

3.3   Results

The comparison between the corpora has enlightened a certain persistence and combination of some linguistics and discursive features, at a micro- as well as a macro-level. At a micro-level, the analysis has shown a remarkable use of the deictic pronoun "*we*". At a macro-level, the two main discursive constructions adopted by the speakers to address the audience are the indirect speech and the storytelling. Here the pronoun "*we*" is alternated, especially in the French corpus, with some nominal designation in order to identify the social group the speaker is siding with. The selection of the social groups to name in the tweets is influenced by the current events in the news. Since the pronoun "*we/nous*" is a function word with a deictic component (i.e. the identification of the designed reality requires a reference to the context of the speech act), we have decided to pay special attention to its analysis in order to investigate the discursive implications of this choice, before putting this pronoun and the nominal syntagms into the complex perspective of the discursive constructions.

3.3.1 The Pronoun "We" and its Discursive Counterparts

Let's consider the actors' designation in the following sentences:

1. NF our Green Prime Minister is clearly determined to despoil our wonderful seascapes. What happens when the wind stops blowing? (October 2020)
2. NF "Boris and his Government are doing as they please without any opposition and we should be very concerned." (September 2020)

3. MLP Voir ce que <u>nos</u> dirigeants ont laissé faire de <u>notre</u> si beau pays fend le cœur… MLP #Dijon #Grésilles (June 2020)[2]
4. MLP <u>Notre</u> pays sombre dans le chaos ! Que fait @Ccastaner ? (June 2020)[3]

The use of "*we*" pronoun and of the deriving forms (the possessive adjectives) is here associated to actions or states of mind the addresser is experiencing as a patient. If emotional states are by definition a condition that affects the subject, the same framework can be applied to some actions or situations the people are undergoing in coercive or non-arbitrary fashion, such as all the decisions taken by representative of the *they*-group: the prime minister, the government, the political leaders ("*nos dirigeants*"), minister Castaner. Without further specifications about the nature of this group, the patient referred to by the first person of the plural can easily be identified with the so-called people or the nation. In all these cases, by choosing a deictic pronoun related to the first person of the plural, the populist politicians convey the impression of aligning their position and their views with the ones of common people, in contrast with the ideas and decisions of the ruling party which represents the establishment. This attempt has nevertheless an argumentative function rather than a referential one, since the politicians cannot indeed be sure of what people really think. We can argue that, by the discursive appropriation of this collective designation, they are exploiting an empathic linguistic structure with the purpose to orientate and frame people's view as well as presenting their opinions as coinciding with his/her own (Rabatel, 2003, 2004). In so doing, they are providing a specific focus on reality and implying that it is shared by the majority—if not everybody—in the country, since the use of "*we*" actually edulcorates the speaker's subjectivity into a collectivity. Thus, the use of the deictic expression can be regarded as a rhetoric strategy that exploits the impression of an empathic connection to shape and impose a certain vision (and interpretation) of reality. By adopting the point of

---

[2]To see what our leaders have done of our beautiful country is heart-breaking….#dijon #Grésilles

[3]Our country is falling into chaos! What is @Ccastaner doing?

view of the addresser/narrator, the reader/addressee participates in the interactive and fluid dynamics of the *ethos*, which is simultaneously the image the speaker wishes to convey according to its will as well as to the expectations he/she attributes to the addressee.

3.3.2   The Use of Indirect and Represented Speech

Indirect speech can assume different forms: there can be reported speech, where the core sentence is introduced by a verb of saying or thinking, or there can be representation of someone else's speech (Rabatel, 2003). Reported speech related to the people (*we*-group) and not to their opponents (*they*-group) is almost absent in our corpus: only one occurrence has been detected in Marine Le Pen's discourse.

Conversely, the representation of people's speech, meaning their feeling and thoughts is dominant. Here are some examples:

5. NF When the Churchill statue and Cenotaph were defaced, this government didn't say a word. We expect better than that from our leaders. (September 2020)
6. NF The establishment are trying to delay the Brexit process. People are getting angry about it. (March 2017)
7. MLP La Présidence de l'Assemblée n'est pas vraiment à l'image du renouvellement qu'attendaient les Français (March 2017)[4]
8. MLP C'était il y a 5 ans, c'est comme si c'était hier. Les attentats du **#13novembre2015** ont laissé en nous tous un traumatisme terrible. Plus que jamais, notre devoir, pour eux tous et leurs proches, c'est l'intransigeance totale et la combativité face à la barbarie islamiste (November 2020)[5].

The underlined sentences and clauses can be rephrased as follows:

---

[4]The Presidency of the Assemblée does not really resemble to what the French people were expecting.

[5]It was five years ago, it is like it was yesterday. The terror attack of #13novembre2015 has left us with a terrible trauma. Even more today, our duty, for them all and for their loved ones, is total intransigence and combativeness against Islamic barbary.

5. We say we are expecting better than that from our leaders.
6. People say they are getting angry about it.
7. The French say that they were expecting…
8. We say that the terror attack of 13th November has left us with a terrible trauma….

This rephrasing operation shows the possibility of placing a verb of speech before the underlined sentences by maintaining some syntactical subject or, in the cases of sentence n° 8, by placing the personal pronoun ("*nous*" = "*we*"), already present as an object, in the subject position. In so doing, this quick test reveals a correspondence between the syntactical subject of the verb of speech and the source of the knowledge conveyed, since it shows how the point of view of people has been embedded in the sentence.

The position and the attitude of the speaker towards the content of these tweets are expressed differently according to the type of designation which is used: the deictic pronoun or the naming of a category. The speaker is either reporting the main content of someone else's ("*people*", "*Français*") statements (6 and 7), either she/he is sharing their view and speaking for a collectivity when she/he uses the *we* pronoun (5 and 8).

It should be noted that, as in the examples presented in the previous section, the verbs associated to these people mainly express emotions or psychological states (Plantin, 2003). The conditions described are distressful and/or painful (the anger, the trauma) and the represented addressee is a passive subject of the situation (the verb to wait and to expect, the expression "*living with trauma*", the fact of being angry). In this regard, the use of the "*we/nous*" pronouns in indirect speech confirms the results we have presented above, about the aligning between the speaker's point of view with common people's opinion.

On the contrary, the study of the designation of the social groups requires some further insight. In the cases were specific social groups are targeted, a double addressing act is performed (Kerbrat-Orecchioni, 2005; Siess & Valency, 2002): while speaking to the wider audience of the followers, the addresser name and depict a specific category in order to speak about its situation. This particular angle shows that the speaker is adopting the point of view of the represented addressee towards the difficulties. In discursive terms, this means he/she is adopting a particular form of indirect speech, the represented speech (Rabatel, 2003), which consists in picturing somebody else's point of view. Given the double address structure, the attempt to establish an empathic connection is not limited only to the represented addressees, but it is enlarged to the broader audience of the Twitter users, who reads this representation and understand that the speaker is siding with the common people. Thus, this impression of empathic connection is simultaneously conveyed to the two audiences: directly to social category mentioned, indirectly to all the potential voters scrolling the Twitter profile.

3.3.3 Short Storytelling Events

Another way to frame reality and englobe the addressee is via storytelling structures. Storytelling messages are composed by series of actions, as in the following examples:

9. NF We're leaving the EU and getting our independence back! (March 2017)
10. NF When we leave the EU, we will be in charge of our own destinies and will have power as individuals to shape our future once again (March 2017).
11. MLP Pillages à #SaintMartin par des bandes armées: le recul de l'Etat et l'impréparation du gouvernement mettent en danger nos compatriotes (March 2017).[6]
12. MLP Les Français doivent pouvoir bénéficier d'une monnaie nationale, qui s'adapte à notre économie et serve nos intérêts (March 2017).[7]
13. MLP Un professeur décapité pour avoir présenté les caricatures de #CharlieHebdo : nous en sommes, en France, à ce niveau de barbarie

---

[6]Pillages in #SaintMartin by armed gangs: the backing of the State and the unprepared government are putting in danger our fellow citizens.

[7]The French must benefit from a national currency, which suits our economy and our interests.

insoutenable. L'islamisme nous mène une guerre: c'est par la force que nous devons le chasser de notre pays (October 2020).[8]

These tweets can be considered as storytelling events since the actions that are selected are not casual but imply a logical and chronological order: cognitive science has in fact shown that narration is a mental process used to make sense and order human experience (Turner, 1996).

This logical organization has been widely studied by semioticians. For the present study, we refer to the narrative macro-sequence theorized by Larivaille (1974), on the basis of Propp's (1965) and Greimas' work (1966), and later contextualized in the linguistic field by Jean-Michel Adam (1994, 2008). According to Larivaille's model, the narrative structure is divided into five phases: (I) the initial situation; (ii) its alteration by a disruptive event that generates the quest (the state of need); (iii) the series of actions and reactions aimed to solve the problem caused by this event and complete the quest; (iv) the climax, i.e. the main and final action that results from the previous series of acts and is meant to solve the problem created by the destabilizing event (v) the final situation, where a new state of things and balance in relationships is established. Due to the limitation of characters number imposed by the media, these sentences show different and selected stages of the narrative process/macro-sequence. Each tweet puts emphasis on the final results, and some of them associate this outcome with the end of the quest or of the troubled situation (10, 12, 13). Example 13 actually presents a more articulated series of actions: there is the disruptive event and the alteration of a previous state (decapitation and level of brutality), the consequences that open the actions/reactions part (the war declared by Islam and the necessity to respond firmly) and the climax (get them, the enemy, out of the country).

The storytelling techniques help the localization—and the inclusion—of the reader/addressee in the anecdotical event which is evoked in the tweet. The adoption of a specific point of view actually facilitates the

---

[8]A school professor was beheaded because he had shown #CharlieHebdo cartoons: we have reached, herein France, this level of intolerable barbary. Islamism is at war against us: it is by mean of strength that we must kick them out of our country.

mental process related to the comprehension of events, and, ultimately, to the meaning-making out of reality.

In these storytelling structures, the use of pronoun "*we*" and of its derivatives are presented as the main sources of the point of view, whether they are active subjects (Nigel Farage's tweets) or passive victims (Marine Le Pen's tweets). This use suggests again that the politicians/speakers are exploiting the processes of empathic connection via the discursive structure of storytelling, by giving the impression that they experience the same situations as common people and that they understand their needs and feelings.

The opponents to the quests may vary according to the contexts: Nigel Farage evokes Europe as the backlash to UK freedom and independence, while Marine Le Pen, is targeting the government, which is unable to connect with the real needs of the common French people or immigration and the Islamic community. In both cases, the narration is framing the *we vs them* logic typical of the populist discourse.

4   Conclusion

The features underlined describe the positioning practice of these two populist politicians. Rather than finding differences, the comparative analysis has shown the recurrence of some features and strategies across the bilingual corpus. Generally speaking, the two politicians tend to adopt the potential voter's point of view, to prove that they are moved by the same feeling and they share the same experiences. Moreover, they try to assimilate with voters, positioning themselves at the same level as the people and underling their strangeness to the elite. This positioning practice is based on the exploitation of the empathic connection to prove to voters that they are like them: common people. This conveyed proximity is used as the basis to get around the idea that they are qualified to represent them, since they belong to the same social environment.

This insistence on the empathic connection has two main discourse consequences: 1. it fills the void left by the absence of factual and logical argumentation; 2. it erases part of the pre-existing *ethos* of the politician (social position, wealth, upbringing). In so doing, part of the speaker's identity is dimmed for the benefit of the "common person" image.

In conclusion, the overall image constructed and projected in this kind of discourses with reference to this digital context can be resumed by the "spokesperson" character, the one that not only shares experiences and values with the crowd but also rises to the position where she/he can speak for that community in the political arena or via social media.

References

Achard-Bayle, G. & Paveau, M. (2012). Réel, contexte et cognition. Contribution à une histoire de la linguistique cognitive. *Histoire Épistémologie Langage, 34*(1), 97–114.

Adam, J. (1994). *Le texte narratif*. Paris: Nathan Université.

Adam, J. (2008 [2005]). *La linguistique textuelle, introduction à l'analyse textuelle des discours*. Paris: Armand Colin.

Amossy, R. (2010). *La présentation de soi: Ethos et identité verbale*. Paris: PUF.

Banfield, A. (1979). *Phrases sans parole*. Paris: Seuil.

Bateson, G. (1980). *Vers une écologie de l'esprit. Tome 2* (Trans. F. Drosso, Laurencine Lot et Eugène Simion). Paris: Seuil.

Benveniste, É. (2011 [1966]). *Problèmes de linguistique générale* (Vol. I). Paris: Gallimard.

Benveniste, É. (2011 [1974]). *Problèmes de linguistique générale* (Vol. II). Paris: Gallimard.

Berthoz, A., & Jorland, G. (2004). *L'empathie*. Paris: Odile Jacob.

Brunel, M.-L., & Cosnier, J. (2014). *L'empathie*. Un sixième sens: Presses Universitaires de Lyon.

Charaudeau, P. (2014). *Le discours politique. Les masque du pouvoir*. Limoges: Lambert-Lucas.

Decety, J. (2004). Neurosciences: les mécanismes de l'empathie, interview with Gaëtanne Chapelle in *Sciences Humaines*, 150.

Decety, J. (2005). Une anatomie de l'empathie. *PSN Psychiatrie, Sciences Humaines, Neurosciences, 3*(11), 16–24.

De Waal, F. (2010). L'Âge de l'empathie: leçons de nature pour une société plus apaisée (trad. de l'anglais). Paris: Éditions Les Liens qui libèrent.

Engesser, S., Ernst, N., Esser, F., & Büchel, F. (2017). Populism and social media: how politicians spread a fragmented ideology. *Information, Communication & Society, 20*(8), 1109–1126.

Ernst, N., Engesser, S., Büchel, F., Blassnig, S., & Esser, F. (2017). Extreme parties and populism: an analysis of Facebook and Twitter across six countries. *Information, Communication & Society, 20*(9), 1347–1364.

Gibson, J. (1979). *The ecological approach to visual perception* (Classic ed.). Boston: Houghton Mifflin.

Greimas, A. J. (2007 [1966]). *Sémantique structurale*. Paris: PUF.

Guilbert, T. (2014). Introduction: articuler les approches qualitatives et quantitatives dans l'analyse du discours. In *Corela*, HS-15. http://corela.revues.org/3545.

Hutchins, E. (1995). How a cockpit remembers its speeds. *Cognitive Science, 19,* 265–288.

Kerbrat-Orecchioni, C. (2005). *Le discours en interaction*. Paris: Armand Colin.

Kleiber, G. (1997). Sens, référence et existence: que faire de l'extra-linguistique? *Langages, 127,* 9–37.

Krämer, B. (2017). Populist online practices: The function of the Internet in right-wing populism. *Information, Communication & Society, 20*(9), 1293–1309.

Kriesi, H. (2014). The populist challenge. *West European Politics, 37*(2), 361–378.

Lakoff, G. (2008). *Political mind*. London: Viking.

Larivaille, P. (1974). L'analyse (morpho) logique du récit. *Poétique, 19,* 368–388.

Maingueneau, D. (1999 [1994]). *L'énonciation en linguistique française*. Paris: Hachette supérieur.

Maingueneau, D. (2009). Auteur et image d'auteur en analyse du discours in *Argumentation et Analyse du Discours*. http://aad.revues.org/660.

Maingueneau, D. (2014). *Discours et analyse du discours*. Paris: Armand Colin.

Mitropoulou, E., & Pignier, N. (2014). Introduction: Interroger les supports? Matières, formes et corps. *Communications et Langages, 182,* 13–28.

Paveau, M.-A. (2012). Ce que disent les objets. Sens, affordance et cognition. In *Synergie* Pays riverains de la baltique, 9. http://gerflint.fr/Base/Baltique9/paveau.pdf.

Paveau, M.-A. (2013). Genre de discours et technologie discursive. Tweet, twittécriture et twittérature. *Pratiques, 157/158,* 7–30.

Peraya, D. (1998). Une révolution sémiotique. *Cahiers Pédagogiques, 362,* 26–28.

Pinotti, A. (2016). *L'empathie. Histoire d'une idée de Platon au posthumain*. Paris: Vrin translated by Sophie Burdet.

Plantin, C. (2003). Structures verbales de l'émotion parlée et de la parole émue. In J.-M. Colletta, & A. Tcherkassof (Eds.), *Les émotions. Cognition, langage et développement* (pp. 97–130). Liège: Mardaga.

Propp, V. (1970 [1965]). *Morphologie du conte*. Paris: Seuil.

Rabatel, A. (1998). *La construction textuelle du point de vue*. Lausanne-Paris: Delachaux et Niestlé.

Rabatel, A. (2003). Les verbes de perception en contexte d'effacement énonciatif: du point de vue représenté aux discours représentés. *Travaux de linguistique* (pp. 49–88). De Boeck Supérieur: Louvain-la-Neuve et à Paris.

Rabatel, A. (2004). Stratégies d'effacement énonciatif et posture de surénonciation dans le Dictionnaire philosophique de Comte-Sponville. *Langages, 156*, 18–33.

Rabatel, A. (2005). La part de l'énonciateur dans la co-construction interactionnelle des points de vue. In *Marges Linguistiques* (pp. 115–136). https://halshs.archives-ouvertes.fr/halshs-00433337/document.

Rabatel, A. (2008). *Homo narrans* (Vols. 1–2). Limoges: Lambert-Lucas.

Rabatel, A. (2017). *Pour une lecture linguistique et critiques des médias. Empathie, éthique, point(s) de vue*. Limoges: Lambert-Lucas.

Siess, J., & Valency, G. (2002). *La double adresse*. Paris: L'Harmattan.

Strate, L. (2004). A media ecology review. In *Communication Research trend*. CSCC, University of Santa Clara. http://cscc.scu.edu/trends/v23/v23_2.pdf.

Turner, M. (1995). *The literary mind, the origins of thought and language*. New York and Oxford: Oxford University Press.

Of Emotion Terms and E-Implicatures: An Exploratory Study of the Explicit and Implicit Emotional Dimensions in a Corpus of Language Teachers' Newsletters

Polina Shvanyukova

1 Introduction

The present investigation is devoted to the analysis of linguistic resources employed to construct and convey the narrator's emotional stance in a small-scale corpus of newsletters in English, published by and for the benefit of the members of the International Association of Teachers of English as a Foreign Language (IATEFL). The bimonthly newsletter *Voices* is the main regular publication produced by the association. Issued in the format of a magazine, *Voices* contains news about recent and future conferences and other events, together with longer feature articles and shorter columns, written by individual IATEFL members. As such, the newsletter provides a space where members can share stories of challenges and opportunities from their own experience of working as

P. Shvanyukova (✉)
Department of Foreign Languages, Literatures and Communication Studies, University of Bergamo, Bergamo, Italy

© The Author(s), under exclusive license to Springer Nature Switzerland AG 2021
P. Anesa and A. Fragonara (eds.), *Discourse Processes between Reason and Emotion*, Postdisciplinary Studies in Discourse,
https://doi.org/10.1007/978-3-030-70091-1_8

English language teaching professionals, and read about stories of others involved in the same professional practice.

The practice of sharing narratives of personal and professional experience has long been recognized to be an important component and tool for teacher reflection, as well as professional and personal identity development (Varghese et al., 2005; Warren, 2020). In language teacher education specifically, research on narratives of professional experience produced by language teachers has highlighted "the use of narrative [as] the predominant means of getting at what teachers know, what they do with what they know and the sociocultural contexts within which they teach and learn to teach" (Golombek & Johnson, 2004: 308).[1] The social process of sharing stories and examples, as Gray (2004) has shown, can boost enculturation of newcomers into the professional practice, stimulate the development of individual and collective identities and help practitioners make sense of their work. Moreover, storytelling can be used as a form of professional dialogue that aims to support the construction of language teachers' professional knowledge (Savvidou, 2010).

In narrative-based research on teachers' knowledge sharing practices, three distinct dimensions of this knowledge have been identified as relational, moral and emotional (Golombek & Johnson, 2004). Narratives, Golombek and Johnson argue, "demonstrate how teachers' knowledge is bound up in how teachers create instruction in response to their emotions and values, and how they place themselves in relation to others" (2004: 308). Golombek and Johnson's (2004) investigation into the role of narrative inquiry as a mediator for teachers' professional development has shown that emotions represent a driving factor in teacher development. Their research has suggested that there exists "an interwoven connection between cognition and emotion, which drives teachers to search for mediational tools to help them externalise their experiences throughout their careers" (Golombek & Johnson, 2004: 323). However, in narrative-based inquiries such as Golombek and Johnson's (2004), the analytical interest lies in the intersections between the emotional, ethical, and relational components of teacher knowledge. The specific linguistic

---

[1] See Warren (2020: 401–405) for an overview of literature on the role of narratives in language teacher education.

choices narrators make and the linguistic resources they rely on in reconstructing their emotional experience and conveying emotional meanings fall outside the scope of narrative-based inquiries. This exploratory study aims to further our understanding of the practice of sharing narratives of personal and professional experience by focusing on patterns of conventional displaying of emotion through linguistic means in language teachers' narratives. More specifically, I will be concerned with the ways in which references to emotions in these texts function as "rhetoric devices that orient an audience towards a [specific] perspective" (Bamberg, 1997: 214). I will start by analysing the range and usage patterns of explicitly emotive or expressive lexical items employed to signal the narrator's emotional stance. Secondly, I will set out to test the validity of the notion of e-implicature (Schwarz-Friesel, 2010) as an analytical tool for the study of implicitly conveyed emotional meanings of texts. As such, this investigation aims to make a contribution towards raising awareness of the potential of making emotion research in linguistics a mainstream practice.

2   Emotion and Language: Theoretical Framework

In the twenty-first century, after the emotional turn has taken place across most social science domains, it is challenging to imagine that the "fundamental human need to express and assess affect" (Ochs & Schieffelin, 1989: 22) has been to a great extent neglected in Western tradition. As Lüdtke (2015) reminds us, the rationalistic conceptualization of language in Western thought has its origins in the tripartite separation of language as *logos*, language as *mythos*, and language as *pathos*. In this separation, the status of "true, propositional, rational, referential, logical, objective and abstract" (Lüdtke, 2015: viii) language was accorded only to language as *logos*, which was elevated above both language of *mythos* and language as *pathos*. From this rationalistic paradigm of *Logos*, the paradigmatic trajectory evolved in linguistics only when an "Emotional Turn" occurred in the second half of the twentieth century (Lüdtke, 2015: viii). This twentieth-century paradigmatic shift was prompted by an emerging conceptualization of language as a representation of reality that is not only true, direct or objective, but subjective as well. In Lüdtke's (2015: viii) sketch of a two-thousand-year-long transition "from rationalistic towards an emotion-integrating conceptualisation of language", the final stage is signalled by the advent of "an Emotion-Integrating Paradigm". With the reinstatement of the complementarity of the two sides of language, the transition from *logos* to *dialogue* has ultimately been accomplished.

As Alba-Juez so succinctly sums it up, "emotions in text (as in life in general) can be very slippery and quite intangible phenomena" (2018: 246). It is beyond the scope of this contribution to review the multiple attempts that have been undertaken in recent years in the fields of psychology, neuroscience, anthropology, social sciences, as well as in linguistics, to produce an all-encompassing definition of emotional phenomena.[2] However, it is still necessary to provide a relevant and comprehensive working definition of what emotions are that will be used as a starting point for the present investigation. Such a definition, I argue, is offered by Schwarz-Friesel (2007):

> Emotions are multi-dimensional, internally represented and subjectively experienced syndrome categories; they can be self-perceived by an individual on the introspective planes of the mind as well as the body; their experiential values are associated with a positive or negative judgement; and they can be expressed to others in the form of perceptible display variants. The judgmental processes concern evaluations through which an individual appraises his/her own bodily sensations, psychological state, behavioural impulses, cognitive representations or general environmental states (in the broadest sense). (Schwarz-Friesel, 2007: 55, translated by and quoted in Langlotz & Locher, 2013: 90)

This definition encompasses the different dimensions of the multi-faceted nature of emotional phenomena that are presented, on the one hand, as internal and subjective, and, on the other hand, as external and (made) visible to others. Another important dimension that is brought to the fore in Schwarz-Friesel's definition involves the evaluative component

---

[2]A recent useful review on the topic is offered in Alba-Juez and Mackenzie (2019).

that extends to the appraisal not only of extraneous, physical manifestations of emotional states, but to the cognitive and contextual planes of perceptions as well.

There is no shortage of useful reviews on the state-of-the-art linguistic research on emotion. Langlotz and Locher (2017), Alba-Juez and Larina (2018), and Alba-Juez and Mackenzie (2019), to name but some of the most recent examples, offer a detailed review of an array of theoretically and methodologically diverse linguistic approaches to the study of emotion (al) talk.[3] In what follows, I will review some of the most relevant linguistic research on emotion in language that will enable me to set up a more specific agenda for the present investigation.

2.1   (Im)Politeness Theory and Emotions

One theoretical framework that appears to have been particularly productive in setting up an agenda and devising methodological toolkits for the description of emotion processes in language is that of (im)politeness theory, as exemplified in both first-wave and second-wave (im)politeness studies.[4] An example of a study that can be positioned within this (second-wave) theoretical orientation is Langlotz and Locher's

---

[3]In Bednarek's (2008) large-scale investigation of the use of linguistic resources for emotion talk in different varieties of British English, emotion terms are defined as "lexical item[s] that [denote] emotion in a broad sense, namely affect, feelings, emotional states, moods, and so on" (Bednarek, 2008: 17). In the same study, Bednarek proposes to distinguish between emotion talk and emotional talk by associating the former with the experiential function of language and the latter with the interpersonal function as described within the theoretical framework of Systemic Functional Linguistics (Halliday, 1973, 1978).

[4]The distinction between first-wave and second-wave politeness research can be traced to an important theoretical distinction between first-order, or lay conceptualisations of politeness, and second-order theoretical conceptualisations of the phenomenon that was introduced by Watts, Sachiko, and Konrad (1992: 3). Taavitsainen and Jucker (2020: 5) clarify that "[f]irst-order concepts are those that members of a speech community use to talk about politeness and interaction, for instance. [...] Second-order concepts, on the other hand, are defined by scholars as analytical tools and in order to delimit as precisely as possible the phenomenon under analysis". As such, studies that take Brown and Levinson's theory of politeness as their point of departure are routinely described as exemplifying the first wave of politeness theory, while studies focusing on first-order politeness, or the discursive politeness analysis, represent the so-called second wave of politeness studies.

$(2013)^5$ investigation in which the extent of the emotional impact on relational work is explored within the framework of the discursive study of politeness. First of all, it is important to note that this theoretical perspective is incompatible with the universalist view of human emotionality that rests on biological foundations (cf. Ekman, 1973, 2003; Plutchik, 2003). The incompatibility derives from the conceptualization of interpersonal relationships as dynamic and discursively constructed in situated interactional practices, in which the interplay between distinct cultural practices and particular cultural norms "[shapes] emotional interpretations in agreement with the social roles that are performed by the interactants" (Langlotz & Locher, 2013: 91). Thus, the emotional component comes to play an important role in situated assessments of politeness norms. For example, in assessing how polite or impolite a given utterance is, interactants may "react with emotions to the violations or adherence of personal expectations and social norms" (Langlotz & Locher, 2013: 87). From this perspective, emotional framing and emotional sense-making skills function as tools the interactants leverage in an attempt to make sense of their communicative actions (Langlotz & Locher, 2013: 89). Hence emotional cues become pragmatic meaning-making resources that are employed to discursively construct and negotiate interpersonal relationships.

This theoretical orientation appears to align with earlier research on the relationship between language and emotion. For example, in a 1997 study Bamberg already proposed to interpret emotions as "indexes for how a person wants to be understood", specifying that "the same emotion term might mean different things in different contexts; and similarly, in particular contexts, other language forms might have the same 'meaning' as emotion terms" (Bamberg, 1997: 212).[6]

However, Langlotz and Locher also offer an important observation on the possibility interactants may exploit of display emotion in ways that

---

[5]See also Locher and Langlotz (2008), Langlotz and Locher (2012), and Locher and Koenig (2014).

[6]In a more recent study, Alba-Juez (2018) develops this line of inquiry in her conceptualisation of emotion "as a response to specific evaluations of the discourse situation and therefore not as a single unified phenomenon, but as part of the intersubjective relational work of the interlocutors" (Alba-Juez, 2018: 232).

are not marked, salient or obvious. In their formulation, "the signalling of evaluations through emotional displays is present in any interactional speech event although such displays may evade our attention because they often remain unmarked" (Langlotz & Locher, 2013: 104). As such, Langlotz and Locher's elucidation comes to complicate Platin's earlier statement on how emotional displays are dependent on the specific situation or genre: "[i]n some speech situations and genres, feelings must be controlled and hidden; in others, disclosing one's feelings is quasi compulsory" (Plantin, 2004: 271).

2.2   Emotional Inferencing

In addition to the theoretical perspective offered by the discursively oriented studies of politeness, I will also draw on research that focuses on the pragmatic phenomenon of emotional inferencing. While the term *e-implicature* has been coined by Schwarz-Friesel (2010), it will be useful to briefly review some earlier research on emotional inferencing to better contextualize Schwarz-Friesel's extensive work on emotion in language from the cognitive linguistic perspective. For example, Ungerer (1997) acknowledged that "[t[he problem for the linguist is that while described emotion can be pinpointed in a text quite accurately, it is much more difficult to get to grips with the emotion that is actually invoked in the reader" (Ungerer, 1997: 309). In order to address this challenge, Ungerer set out to devise a systematic methodological framework for the analysis of possible emotional reactions that a text could trigger in a reader. His proposal was to make use of Grice's notion of inference understood "as a rational process conducted by the hearer of comparing the linguistic input with the maxims and extracting its informational content"[7] (Ungerer, 1997: 310), which Ungerer adapted to describe what he called "the reader's *emotional inferences*" (1997: 310, original emphasis). In reconfiguring Grice's notion of inference for the analysis

---

[7]Cf. Horn's definition of implicature as "a component of speaker meaning that constitutes an aspect of what is **meant** in a speaker's utterance without being part of what is **said**. What a speaker intends to communicate is characteristically far richer than what she directly expresses; linguistic meaning radically underdetermines the message conveyed and understood" (Horn, 2007: 3, original emphasis).

of emotional reactions, Ungerer drew on Brown and Levinson's influential descriptive framework for politeness phenomena. By integrating a new component of emotional associations to the supposedly rational process of decoding of politeness strategies as described by Brown and Levinson, Ungerer was able to develop a pragmatic methodology for the study of emotional inferencing based on a set of inferencing principles (Ungerer, 1997: 313–319). Ungerer's specific concern, however, was with the emotional impact of news stories, and the methodological toolkit that was developed in his study has been mainly applied for the analysis of this particular textual genre.

The argument that emotions can be conveyed not only explicitly, by employing a wide range of linguistic resources, but also implicitly, that is to say, through ideational meanings, represents the core of Schwarz-Friesel's (2007, 2010, 2015, 2019) innovative work on e-implicatures. Schwarz-Friesel introduces the notion of emotive implicatures, or e-implicatures, to refer to pragmatic (and conceptual) implicatures about the emotions of the speaker that are based, to a certain degree, on culturally shaped encyclopaedic knowledge (Schwarz-Friesel, 2010, 2015). The ability to process the implicit meaning of an utterance or text comes to play a crucial role when dealing especially with "indirect speech acts and texts with referential under-specification" (Schwarz-Friesel, 2015: 169). It is by drawing specific e-implicatures about implicitly conveyed evaluations that interactants make sense of their communicative actions and are able to negotiate their roles in interaction. In other words, Schwarz-Friesel proposes to apply the idea that "linguistically encoded meaning is standardly high underdetermined" also for the emotive language use (Schwarz-Friesel, 2015: 169). As also Alba-Juez (2018) makes it clear, any attempt to assess the emotional content of a text calls for an investigation of not only the microstructure (e.g. specific morpho-lexical items on the lexico-semantic dimension [Schwarz-Friesel, 2015]), but of the relevant pragmatic aspects on the level of macrostructure as well. E-implicature represents one of such relevant pragmatic aspects that warrants further scrutiny on the account of its potential, as an analytical tool, to uncover the attitudes of the interactants and the strategies the interactants employ to negotiate interpersonal relationships in a given social interaction.

This brief review of the relevant literature of the linguistic research on emotion has provided a number of important theoretical and methodological insights that will be applied in the present investigation to the study of the ways in which explicit and implicit emotional meanings are conveyed through linguistic means in newsletters produced by and addressed to the members of a well-established language teacher association.

3   Dataset and Methodology

In Lamb's (2012) study of language teacher associations (LTAs), LTAs are defined as "networks of professionals, run by and for professionals, focused mainly on support for members, with knowledge exchange and development as well as representation of members' views as their defining functions" (Lamb, 2012: 295).[8] According to Lamb, the two main functions of this specific type of professional associations can be identified, respectively, as "the external advocacy function" and "the internal professional development function" (Lamb, 2012: 289). The former reflects the role associations play as expert advocates of their subjects that can influence policymakers and the general public, while the latter highlights their function of supporting and fostering their members' professional development (Lamb, 2012: 288).

As Lamb points out, the internal professional function encompasses a number of more restricted sub-functions, such as, for example, the knowledge dissemination sub-function that focuses on facilitating information exchange about and development of effective professional practice (Lamb, 2012: 295). At the same time, LTAs' endeavours in enhancing professional development are not limited to the routines of the sharing of practical knowledge. Most importantly, these professional associations play a key role in "reinforcing the values, beliefs and identity of the profession" (Lamb, 2012: 289).

---

[8]Lamb's study was carried out as part of a larger collaborative project on Language Associations and Collaborative Support (LACS) conducted by the European Centre for Modern Languages (ECML) and the Fédération Internationale des Professeurs de Langues Vivantes/International Federation of Language Teacher Associations (FIPLV) (Lamb, 2012: 287).

My case-study in this investigation is represented by an LTA that has been an influential stake-holder in the field of English Language Teaching since 1967. The International Association of Teachers of English as a Foreign Language (IATEFL), according to the official website of the association (https://www.iatefl.org/about), "has been linking, developing and supporting English language teaching professionals worldwide [for over 50 years]". IATEFL (from my own experience of being a member of the association) actively promotes knowledge and expertise exchange between its members, as well as interaction (online and in person) for social purposes. As such, the association can be said to represent a successful example of a community of practice[9] that brings together English language teaching professionals from all around the world.

IATEFL fulfils its "internal professional development function" by organizing a variety of events (https://www.iatefl.org/events), by encouraging members to become part of one of the sixteen different Special Interest Groups (SIGs, https://www.iatefl.org/special-interests) and by producing a number of publications addressed to its members. Thus, IATEFL represents an example of a self-organizing system of informal learning and, as such, it is shared learning and interest to keep it together as a community of people "with a shared domain of expertise who voluntarily learn together about practices that matter to them" (Gray, 2004: 22).

IATEFL's main regular publication is a bimonthly newsletter *Voices*. *Voices* provides a space for IATEFL members to share stories of challenges and opportunities from their own experience of working as English language teaching professionals. For the present investigation, twelve issues of the newsletter covering the period between March-April 2018 (Issue 261) and January-February 2020 (Issue 272) were analysed by adopting a combination of qualitative and quantitative approaches.

In the first phase of the investigation, the analysis relied on corpus linguistic techniques, applied to the self-compiled corpus of ca. 250,000

---

[9]As is well known, Wenger et al. define a community of practice (CoP) as "[a group] of people who share a concern, a set of problems, or a passion about a topic, and who deepen their knowledge and expertise in this area by interacting on an ongoing basis" (Wenger, McDermott, & Snyder, 2002: 4).

tokens containing electronic versions of the twelve issues of the maga-zine. Frequency lists and keywords were analysed in order to detect the presence of specific linguistic means employed to signal the different emotional states. This quantitative analysis confirmed Oster's (2010) findings about the tendency of emotion words to be low frequency words.[10]

The search for specific lemmas, including a selection of emotion terms extracted from Bednarek's (2008) list of emotion terms in British English, was more productive. Finally, the analysis focused on a number of concordance lines containing the relevant lexical items that were inspected manually.[11] In what follows, I will illustrate the main findings of this exploratory study by discussing some examples extracted from the corpus.

4   Analysis

4.1   The Use of Explicit Emotional Lexis

The manual inspection of a number of selected concordance lines containing the relevant lexical items shows that the use of emotion terms to explicitly disclose the narrator's emotional stance represents an impor-tant strategy employed by the narrators to discursively construct and negotiate their relationship with the audience of potential readers. As examples (1), (2) and (3) show, emotional lexis can be introduced to describe one's emotional state in simple emotive propositions (1) or in rhetorical questions addressed directly at the reader ([2] and [3]):

(1) As an ELT teacher, teacher educator and consultant, I love language. (*Voices* 271, 5)

---

[10]Olster here discusses the challenges of a corpus-based analysis of the linguistic expression of emotion concepts and draws our attention to "the methodological difficulty of finding an adequate balance between semi-automatic and manual analysis" (Oster, 2010: 755).

[11]For the retrieval of the frequency and keyword lists I used #LancsBox version 4.0. The same software was used to retrieve the concordance lines for the manual analysis.

(2) Have you ever been worried about introducing controversial subjects into your classroom? A Polish born teacher from Greece, Margarita Kosior, presented the group with a simple yet powerful tool to broach difficult subjects in the classroom such as modern-day slavery, racism and even homosexuality. 'My advice is not to be afraid. [...]' (*Voices* 261, 4)

(3) If you are a non-native teacher of English, how would you feel if you were invited to teach English in the United Kingdom?

This was exactly what happened to me even before I left Brazil. I received an email from a very well-known language institute in Cambridge explaining they had received my CV via a former student and asking me if I would like to teach teenagers in their summer course. I was pleased and surprised for a number of reasons—first, because an acquaintance had recommended me without my knowledge, but mainly because moving countries generated a lot of insecurity regarding my professional future in the UK. I believe many non-native EFL teachers would feel insecure in the same situation. (*Voices* 265, 3)

In the two longer examples ([2] and [3]), we can observe how the narrative evolves by invoking a series of changing emotional states in a progression (from worry/anxiety to fear in [2]; from satisfaction/surprise to feeling insecure and possibly anxious in [3]). These persuasive emotional sequences engage the reader who is encouraged to relate to these emotional states. A similar progression, in this case of an abrupt transformation from happiness to shock, can be found in example (4):

(4) I was happy with the change and thought that this was just what my learners needed in order to truly make English a second language in their lives. But I got a rude shock when most of them did not respond to the tasks and activities in class. (*Voices* 271, 17)

As can be observed in these four examples, it is quite typical that the first-person narrator in these articles only interrupts her/himself in order to address the potential interlocutor, either explicitly, for example, by making use of the second-person pronoun *you* in rhetorical questions, or indirectly. In (3) we find an example of an indirect address whereby the interlocutor is tentatively invited to identify with the group of "non-native EFL teachers". Another example of an invitation to acknowledge a sense of common identity is provided in example (5):

(5) As teachers, we should be very uncomfortable with the idea that our learners ever feel that aspects of their identity are ignored or delegitimised, and that they subsequently feel that their only recourse is to suffer in silence or challenge the authority of the teacher, the materials, the syllabus and the institution. (*Voices* 272: 6)

The combination of the involved and narrative dimensions typical of feature articles with the emotional component constitutes a set of linguistic meaning-making resources that is employed in these texts to not only discursively construct and negotiate interpersonal relationships between the narrators and their potential readers, but to build and reinforce a sense of belonging to a community of practice.

It is a well-established fact that affective language can be highly figurative (Schwarz-Friesel, 2015). In addition to explicit emotional lexis that was retrieved using a combination of manual and automated methods, the manual inspections of selected passages made it possible to retrieve a number of examples containing figurative or metaphoric language, as shown in examples (6) and (7):

(6) In 2014 at the IATEFL Conference in Harrogate, plenary speaker Jackie Kay read us her autobiographical journey as a lesbian mother looking for her birth father and mother. I was moved to tears listening to her story. (*Voices* 269: 22)

(7) In 1995, with young children now turning into teenagers and looking at university, we decided to make the move back to Europe – a very difficult decision as my role in Iran was not only key but one that I loved, too. But move we did – and after a difficult year in the UK (reverse culture shock completely floored me), we made the decision to move to Spain [...]. (*Voices* 270: 18)

The personal style of writing, however, can be discarded in favour of a more impersonal approach, especially when such sensitive and potentially distressing emotional states as guilt or regret are discussed. As example (8) shows, the narrator chooses to switch from direct address to a more generic denomination "many people" in order to mitigate the potentially distressing impact of this particular passage in the text:

(8) For many people, looking at their personal level of physical disorganisation can cause feelings of guilt, possible regret and, in some cases, almost physical pain. (*Voices* 270: 16)

4.2   Emotional Inferencing

The manual analysis of selected concordance lines also made it possible to retrieve a number of examples from the corpus whose interpretation must necessarily involve the work of emotional inferencing. The examples that will be discussed in this sub-section show how readers can be challenged to engage in the mental reconstruction process in an attempt to access the affective meaning (Schwarz-Friesel, 2015). This can be accomplished by drawing e-implicatures. How challenging the readers may find the process of drawing e-implicatures depends, to a large extent, on whether or not the interactants share the necessary culturally shaped encyclopaedic knowledge.

It appears likely that the readers of *Voices* would easily draw the relevant e-implicatures from examples (9) and (10):

(9) It was interesting to notice how much difference the pedagogical competence or otherwise of the dance teachers made to my experience as a learner. I come away from the 'good' dance lessons feeling energised, successful and motivated to return to the teacher's next lesson. I come away from the 'poor' dance lessons feeling annoyed, frustrated and vowing never again to attend a lesson with that teacher. (*Voices* 271: 6)

(10) My goal was that students would use Quizlet not as a test-cramming tool but as a means of consistently learning the target vocabulary. I wanted the app to complement the vocabulary in the textbook, which

would encourage learner autonomy and reduce teacher instruction. After completing both units, I felt there were some areas for improvement. While I reminded students to use the app, I felt that I could have done a better job in this regard. When I saw the total time that students spent on Quizlet, I felt that they should have spent more. (*Voices* 270: 13)

In example (9), the narrator shares her personal experience of attending a "good" dance class to stimulate a discussion on the importance of pedagogical competence for English language teachers and their language learners. The mental reconstruction challenge in (9) involves making the right association between an emotionally positive and/or an emotionally negative experience of a learner in a dance class with one's own good or bad teaching practices. What makes example (10) different from (9) is the narrator's decision to not explicitly encode his actual emotional state, which is only hinted at in the repetition of the string *I felt..I felt..I felt*. The reader is thus asked to perform the work of emotional inferencing by drawing on her/his encyclopaedic knowledge of how an English language teacher would be expected to feel in the same situation. Would they feel frustrated and disappointed with themselves? Would they feel that they did not live up not only to their own, but to their students' expectations as well? Or would they simply feel annoyed by having to acknowledge their lack of preparation? These are some of the possible inferences that could be drawn from example (10). It can also be hypothesized that being forced to draw e-implicatures in order to access the affective meaning could potentially help the reader to identify with the narrator in a more meaningful way. This, I believe, would happen if the reader felt compelled to put her/himself into the narrator's shoes and mentally relive what she/he imagined to be the narrator's emotional state.

As this investigation is of an exploratory nature and no quantitative findings can be provided at this stage, only a tentative claim can be made that concerns the predominance of negative emotional states over positive emotional states that require the work of emotional inferencing to reconstruct the affective meaning in this corpus. In the sample of four examples in Sect. 4.2, three of these (examples [10], [11] and [12]) offer descriptions of negative emotional experiences. In addition to

(10) discussed above, excerpt (11) tells the story of one member's frustration with some of IATEFL's policies. The work of emotional inferencing here is facilitated thanks to some rhetorical moves the narrator makes. One such example is the explicit acknowledgement that the possibility of avoiding publishing reps and their products at the annual conference represents a welcome change:

> (11) Having said all of this, it would be unfair to dismiss IATEFL as nothing more than a corporate mouthpiece. As an organisation, it appears to be becoming increasingly aware of the prevalence of corporate ELT at its Conferences. This year, the confinement of the Exhibition to the basement made it easy to avoid publishing reps trying to sell their products, and the recently adopted practice of highlighting sessions that are sponsored by publishers meant that you could go through the entire Conference without having a single book or digital product shoved down your throat. This makes a welcome change from previous years. (*Voices* 269: 11)

Arguably, the work of emotional inferencing becomes more challenging in (12):

> (12) If we turned on the heater in the room, the lights went out and vice versa; attendance was erratic as students were often needed at family medical or asylum appointments at short notice or because students couldn't get into the communal bathroom at any other time and missed class to bathe or wash their hair; I missed having the technology I was used to and, with no access to my IWB or Google images, had to draw and mime as best as I could. (*Voices* 263: 4)

This extract is taken from a member's story of her experience of volunteering as a teacher for children living in a refugee camp. What is striking about this text is how sparingly conventional emotional lexis is used throughout the entire text of this moving narrative. With none or little help on the level of the microstructure of the text, the reader is challenged to activate her/his encyclopaedic knowledge in order to fully experience the intensity of the narrator's emotional state.

5   Concluding Remarks

This exploratory study investigated patterns of conventional displaying of emotion through linguistic means in language teachers' narratives of personal and professional experience. The analysis of the range and usage patterns of explicitly emotive lexis showed that the use of emotion terms to explicitly disclose the narrator's emotional stance represents a key strategy employed by the narrators to discursively construct and negotiate their relationship with the audience of potential readers. By making their emotional states transparent and easily accessible to others, the narrators share their emotional experiences in a bid to engage the readers and effectively enhance the sense of common identity of global English language teaching professionals. The set of linguistic meaning-making resources the narrators rely on in order to reinforce the sense of common belonging also includes rhetorical questions and figurative or metaphoric language. At the same time, impersonalization strategies can be applied to mitigate the impact of potentially more distressing narratives of personal experience.

As recently as 2015, Schwarz-Friesel rightly lamented the fact that the emotional turn had had only a minor impact on mainstream linguistics. As a result, the implicit emotional dimension in texts remains an under-researched phenomenon. The present study has attempted to make a contribution towards filling in this research gap. This was done by applying e-implicature as an analytical tool in the investigation of the implicit emotion dimension in language teachers' narratives. The analysis of selected examples showed that performing the work of emotional inferencing in order to access the affective meaning could potentially help the reader to identify with the narrator in a more meaningful way.

However, a major methodological challenge associated with the analysis of emotional inference concerns the necessity of conducting such analysis manually, for example, by examining concordance lines extracted from the corpus. That there exists a potentially infinite number of creative ways of conveying implicit emotional meanings means that the retrieval of such linguistic strings represents a critical challenge for corpus-based investigations of emotion in language. More research is needed to devise and test possible solutions to this critical methodological challenge.

References

Alba-Juez, L. (2018). Emotion and appraisal processes in language: How are they related? In M. los Ángeles Gómez González & J. Lachlan Mackenzie (Eds.), *The construction of discourse as verbal interaction* (pp. 227–250). Amsterdam: John Benjamins.

Alba-Juez, L., & Lachlan Mackenzie, J. L. (2019). Emotion processes in discourse. In J. L. Mackenzie & L. Alba-Juez (Eds.), *Emotion in discourse* (pp. 3–26). Amsterdam: John Benjamins.

Alba-Juez, L., & Larina, T. (2018). Language and emotion: Discourse-pragmatic perspectives. *Russian Journal of Linguistics, 22*(1), 9–37.

Bamberg, M. (1997). Emotion talk(s): The role of perspective in the construction of emotions. In S. Niemeier & R. Dirven (Eds.), *Language of emotions: Conceptualization, expression, and theoretical foundation* (pp. 209–229). Amsterdam: John Benjamins.

Bednarek, M. (2008). *Emotion talk across corpora.* Basingstoke: Palgrave Macmillan.

Ekman, P. (1973). *Darwin and facial expression.* New York: Academic Press.

Ekman, P. (2003). *Emotions revealed: Recognizing faces and feelings to improve communication and emotional life.* New York: Times Books.

Golombek, P. R., & Johnson, K. E. (2004). Narrative inquiry as a mediational space: Examining emotional and cognitive dissonance in second-language teachers' development. *Teachers and Teaching: Theory and Practice, 10*(3), 307–327.

Gray, B. (2004). Informal learning in an online community of practice. *Journal of Distance Education/ Revue de l'Enseignement à Distance, 19*(1), 20–35.

Halliday, M. A. K. (1973). *Explorations in the functions of language.* London: Edward Arnold.

Halliday, M. A. K. (1978). *Language as a social semiotic.* London: Edward Arnold.

Horn, L. R. (2007). Implicatures: Some basic oppositions. In L. R. Horn & G. Ward (Eds.), *The handbook of pragmatics* (pp. 3–28). Oxford: Blackwell.

Lamb, T. (2012). Language associations and collaborative support: Language teacher associations as empowering spaces for professional networks. *Innovation in Language Learning and Teaching, 6*(3), 287–308.

Langlotz, A., & Locher, M. A. (2012). Ways of communicating emotional stance in online disagreements. *Journal of Pragmatics, 44*(12), 1591–1606.

Langlotz, A., & Locher, M. A. (2013). The role of emotions in relational work. *Journal of Pragmatics, 58,* 87–107.

Langlotz, A., & Locher, M. A. (2017). (Im)politeness and emotion. In J. Culpeper, M. Haugh & D. Kádár (Eds.), *The Palgrave handbook of linguistic (im)politeness* (pp. 287–322). London: Palgrave Macmillan.

Locher, M. A., & Koenig, R. (2014). All I could do was hand her another tissue: Handling emotions as a challenge in reflective writing texts by medical students. In A. Langlotz & A. Soltysik Monnet (Eds.), *Emotion, affect, sentiment: The language and aesthetics of feeling* (pp. 215–236). Tübingen: Narr.

Locher, M. A., & Langlotz, A. (2008). Relational work: At the intersection of cognition, interaction and emotion. *Bulletin suisse de linguistique appliquée, 88,* 165–191.

Lüdtke, U. M. (2015). From Logos to Dialogue. In U. M. Lüdtke (Ed.), *Emotion in language: Theory—research—application* (pp. vii–xii). Amsterdam: John Benjamins.

Ochs, E., & Schieffelin, B. (1989). Language has a heart. *Text 9*(1), Special Issue: *The Pragmatics of Affect,* 7–25.

Oster, U. (2010). Using corpus methodology for semantic and pragmatic analyses: What can corpora tell us about the linguistic expression of emotions? *Cognitive Linguistics, 21*(4), 727–763.

Plantin, C. (2004). On the inseparability of reason and emotion in argumentation. In E. Weigand (Ed.), *Emotion in dialogic interaction* (pp. 269–281). Amsterdam: John Benjamins.

Plutchik, R. (2003). *Emotions and life: Perspectives from psychology, biology, and evolution.* Washington: American Psychological Association.

Savvidou, C. (2010). Storytelling as dialogue: How teachers construct professional knowledge. *Teachers and Teaching: Theory and Practice, 16*(6), 649–664.

Schwarz-Friesel, M. (2007). *Sprache und emotion.* Tübingen and Basel: Francke.

Schwarz-Friesel, M. (2010). Expressive Bedeutung und E-Implikaturen – Zur Relevanz konzeptueller Bewertungen bei indirekten Sprechakten: Das Streichbarkeitskriterium und seine kognitive Realität. In W. Rudnitzky (Ed.), *Kultura Kak Tekst (Kultur als Text)* (pp. 12–27). Moscow: SGT.

Schwarz-Friesel, M. (2015). Language and emotion: The cognitive linguistic perspective. In U. Lüdtke (Ed.), *Emotion in Language* (pp. 157–174). Amsterdam: John Benjamins.

Schwarz-Friesel, M. (2019). Emotionalität von Texten aus kognitionslinguistischer Perspektive. In H. Kappelhoff et al. (Eds.), *Emotionen. Ein interdisziplinäres Handbuch* (pp. 403–409). Berlin: Metzler.

Taavitsainen, I., & Jucker, A. H. (2020). Introduction. In A. H. Jucker & I. Taavitsainen (Eds.), *Manners, norms and transgressions in the history of English* (pp. 1–23). Amsterdam: John Benjamins.

Ungerer, F. (1997). Emotions and emotional language in English and German news stories. In S. Niemeier & R. Dirven (Eds.), *Language of emotions: Conceptualization, expression, and theoretical foundation* (pp. 307–328). Amsterdam: John Benjamins.

Varghese, M., Morgan, B., Johnston, B., & Johnson, K. A. (2005). Theorizing language teacher identity: Three perspectives and beyond. *Journal of Language, Identity, and Education, 4*(1), 21–44.

Warren, A. N. (2020). Language teachers' narratives of professional experience in online class discussions. *Text & Talk, 40*(3), 399–419.

Watts, R. J., Sachiko, I., & Konrad, E. (1992). Introduction. In R. J. Watts, S. Ide, & K. Ehlich (Eds.), *Politeness in language: Studies in its history, theory and practice* (pp. 1–17). Berlin: Mouton de Gruyter.

Wenger, E., McDermott, R., & Snyder, W. (2002). *Cultivating communities of practice*. Boston, MA: Harvard University Business School Press.

Index

Printed by Printforce, the Netherlands